BARKING MAD

Book Three

DOG GONE CRAZY

Published in 2026 by Write Laugh Ltd

www.tomemoffatt.com

ISBN 978-1-7386184-8-4 (print)
ISBN 978-1-7386184-9-1 (eBook)

A catalogue record for this book is available from the National Library of New Zealand.

Write Laugh editing team: Anna Bowles & Marj Griffiths
Cover design and illustrations: Paul Beavis
Print and eBook design: Write Laugh

BARKING MAD

Book Three

DOG GONE CRAZY

TOM E. MOFFATT

ILLUSTRATED BY PAUL BEAVIS

To Willow,
the first dog I went crazy over.

CONTENTS

See It to Believe It

I skidded to a halt on Granddad's front porch, leaning one hand on the door as I caught my breath. What did he want help with this time? He'd sounded pretty worried on the phone, his voice fast and urgent.

"Get here as soon as you can! And make sure you ring the doorbell!"

It couldn't be anything too crazy. It wasn't like he was working on a mind-swapping machine or robo-dog these days. Just an electric flea collar for DaVinci. Surely not even Granddad could mess that up.

I slotted my key in the lock and turned it. No point ringing the doorbell when I have my own key. And anyway, I didn't want to miss Granddad's face when he saw how quickly I'd got there.

Click.

Barking broke out in the distance, getting closer and louder.

I pushed the door open. If I waited until DaVinci slammed into it, I might never get inside. He's pretty strong, that dog.

And fast.

I could hear the thump of his paws on the carpet as he pelted down the corridor. I glanced around, expecting to see DaVinci's tongue lolling out of the side of his mouth, trailing a streamer of drool. His tail wagging as he bounded along, barking with excitement.

There was none of that. Just the excited barking.

But no dog.

Granddad's voice came from the other room. An urgent shout. The only word I made out was 'doorbell'.

Then BAM!

Something ploughed straight into my groin, folding me in half. I let out an 'Oof!' as I flopped onto the carpet, staring around for the source of the impact.

Still nothing.

Then something wet and warm squelched onto my cheek and slid up over my eyeball.

Eww! What the heck was that?

I wiped my eye on my wrist, then pulled my hand away and examined it. A slimy substance glistened on my skin. It looked like doggy-drool. I should know. I'd been covered in it often enough. But where did it come from?

Granddad staggered into the hallway, bent double, gulping big raspy breaths of air.

"Shut … the … door!" he gasped.

The fear in his voice hit me like a bucket of icy water. And the look on his face. Instead of pleasant surprise, it was utter horror.

I spun around and reached out towards the door.

As I stretched, something crashed into me from behind, launching me forward. My forehead slammed into the door. Pain blossomed from the point of impact and white specks filled my vision, like a firework had just gone off inside my head.

Ow! Ow! Ow!

When my sight returned I was lying on my back on the porch, Granddad rushing down the hall towards me. "Grab him!" he shouted. "Before he gets away!"

I tried to sit up, looking for someone to grab, but a heavy weight pressed into my thigh. Then my stomach. Then my chest. It was like being flattened by an invisible stampede of cattle.

Something pointy jammed into my cheek, pinning my head to the floor. My mouth slipped open, my tongue encountering earthy-tasting fur. I squeezed my lips shut and covered my face with my hands, bracing myself for another impact.

But nothing happened.

I lowered my arms and looked around, dazed. Like the victim of a hit-and-run. Granddad filled the doorway. He seemed extremely tall from this angle. And I could see white hairs up his nose.

He stepped over me, his old slipper landing on the doorstep beside my ear. Then he bent down and crept forward, his arms exploring the empty air in front of him, like he was blindfolded and didn't want to bump into anything.

I felt the lump above my eyebrow.

"Ow!" I said, sitting up. "What was that?"

Granddad didn't answer. He just kept blindly feeling his way along the garden path, his arms stretched out wide.

I tried again. "Hey, Granddad? Who was I supposed to grab?"

Granddad stopped halfway down the path and turned towards me, frowning with disappointment, like Mrs Higman whenever she handed me back a maths test.

"DaVinci," he said, staring down at the ground. "But you were supposed to ring the doorbell so I could grab him."

"But..." I said, looking around. I didn't get it. Where was that dog? I'd definitely heard him. Heck, I'd even tasted him.

But I didn't see a thing.

A nasty realisation came to me.

"That was..."

"DaVinci. Yes."

"But ... he was..."

"Invisible. Yes."

Granddad stood up straight, his arms flopping to his sides. He suddenly looked older. More tired.

"It was the flea collar," he mumbled. "I set it to maximum vibrate and could literally see the fleas jumping off him. Then I couldn't see anything. DaVinci completely disappeared."

"You mean..." I said, trying to get my head around what Granddad was saying, "the flea collar turned DaVinci invisible?"

Granddad nodded. "He panicked and I couldn't find him anywhere. I figured if you rang the doorbell, he'd come out of hiding to greet you."

Oh, no! Why the heck didn't I follow Granddad's instructions and ring that stupid doorbell?

Now the dog could be anywhere. Doing anything. In fact, he could be doing cartwheels across the lawn right now and we wouldn't have a clue.

And it was all my fault!

2. Park that Thought

After a final glance around the empty street, I followed Granddad to his workshop. We left the front door open in case DaVinci came back on his own for the first time in his disobedient life.

Granddad stood at his workbench, shuffling through random sheets of paper and mumbling unintelligible phrases.

"Molecular vibration inducer..."

"...beyond the visible spectrum."

"...fleas repelled by lower frequency..."

BER
DAD

"But what does that all mean?" I asked, gently rubbing the lump on my forehead again.

Granddad stopped and looked at me with his piercing blue eyes. "It means the vibrations from the collar refract the light at exactly the right frequency to render DaVinci optically undetectable."

I stared back blankly. "Optically undetectable?"

"Invisible."

I shrugged. "Well, at least you got rid of the fleas!" I had to stop myself from adding, 'Along with the rest of the dog!'

Then a thought hit me.

"Is it..." I said, hesitating on the last word. I forced myself to say it. "...permanent?"

DaVinci was hard enough to control when you could see him. The thought of him being invisible for the rest of his life was too much.

"Oh, no," Granddad said, squinting as if I'd just asked if DaVinci liked food. "Only while the collar vibrates."

"And how long will that be?"

Granddad raised his eyebrows and said, "Until the battery runs out."

"And how long will that be?" He seemed determined to make me work for my answers.

"I don't know. It was a fresh battery, so hours. Maybe even days."

Days? An invisible DaVinci roaming the streets. For days.

Oh no.

Granddad really had messed up this time.

DaVinci was terrible at crossing roads. And that's when drivers could see him. And if he did avoid getting run over, what crazy stuff would he get up to if no one could see him coming?

Right.

We had to find him.

But how?

It's not like we could put up a 'Lost Dog' poster. It would just be a blank sheet of paper saying, 'Have you seen this dog?'

I looked to Granddad for support. He stared at his workbench, his hand massaging his forehead, as though trying to iron out the worry lines.

That wasn't going to fix this mess.

We needed a plan.

So ... where would DaVinci go?

He was obviously in a panic, otherwise he wouldn't have charged off. Usually when he runs away, he ends up at the park. In the past, we've always gone to the park, found him causing havoc, then brought him home.

This time, we wouldn't be able to see him.

He could literally be right under our noses and we wouldn't have a clue.

Except for his smell. But we couldn't exactly crawl around town on all fours, sniffing. Hoping to bump up against stinky invisible fur.

No. We'd need to make him come to us.

I went to the coat rack by the back door and found a faded tennis ball with a bald patch and dangly grey strands. Then I grabbed the bag of stale old treats we used to use for doggy-training, before everyone gave it up as a lost cause. Now they're used to bribe him when he's being exceptionally naughty. I also grabbed his lead and the poo bags, both of which often come in handy in the park.

"Granddad?" I said softly, not wanting to startle him out of his million-mile stare. "Are you ready?"

"Wuh?"

We stared at each other for a few seconds, Granddad's wrinkly face moving through the stages of recognition, recall, and shock. He closed his eyes briefly, then opened them and nodded.

"Yes," he said firmly. "Let's have lunch!"

"What ... no!" I held up the lead and the bag of doggy treats, giving both a jiggle. "Let's get in the car and go looking for DaVinci. Before anything worse happens to him."

"Ah, right ... yes," said Granddad slowly, his eyes glazing over again. Perhaps it would be better if I did this alone? But it would take too long searching on foot. And this was all Granddad's fault, so he should help fix it.

Granddad patted various pockets, keys jangling on the third attempt, then slowly made his way towards the front door.

When we got outside, I glanced up and down the street. This was going to be even harder than I'd imagined.

We were literally looking for nothing.

Once we were in Granddad's car, he tootled out of the driveway and headed towards the park. I pressed my face against the window, searching for anything out of the ordinary. But everything was completely in the ordinary.

A little kid zoomed along the pavement on a balance bike, a huge grin on his face.

An old lady tugged at the lead of her tiny sausage dog, which was sniffing the base of a tree.

A man hosed his car down in a driveway, a river of water running into the roadside gutter.

All normal Saturday lunchtime activities.

Then we got to the park and my stomach dropped. Picnics were another normal Saturday lunchtime activity. And there were dozens of them going on. The park was utterly packed.

There were blankets laid out all over the place.

Parents chatting and passing around food.

Kids playing Frisbee.

Games of football.

All the things that get DaVinci excited.

This was going to be a nightmare.

A Sandwich Short of a Picnic

We stood at the entrance to the park, surveying the scene. I'd never seen it busier with all the things that turn DaVinci into a nightmare.

Dogs.

Food.

Balls.

Frisbees.

Ducks.

Kids.

I didn't want to think about the chaos he could cause.

But ... he clearly wasn't here. No one was crying, screaming or fleeing the park in terror. Which they would be doing if invisible DaVinci was sniffing around. But this was a good place to start. With these crowds, we'd know about it as soon as he got here.

Granddad and I headed down the main path, scanning the scenes on either side of us.

To my right, a small boy—only six or seven years old—attempted to throw a Frisbee. He spun his whole body and launched it at a downward angle, making it thump onto the grass and roll off in the opposite direction to his dad. The dad jogged over and picked it up, gently throwing it back, so that it landed at the boy's feet.

To my left, a mum had four plates laid out on a picnic blanket and was sharing out square white-bread sandwiches.

We kept walking, scanning the park for signs of disturbance. Granddad couldn't have gone more slowly if he tried. He hobbled along, stopping to rub his knee every three seconds.

It was painful. And I don't mean his knee.

We eventually reached the duck pond at the end of the path.

A grandmother held on to a toddler's hoodie as the little girl flung huge hunks of bread into the murky water. Ducks flapped and tooted as they jostled to be the lucky winner of a soggy chunk.

I looked at Granddad and he shrugged.

DaVinci wasn't here.

No way.

A well-behaved invisible dog might snooze in the shade of a tree. But not DaVinci. If he was here, he'd be mayhem in motion.

But where else could he have gone?

My house, maybe? Perhaps he was sitting at the front door, waiting for someone to come or go?

School? He'd turned up there once before and sent the entire playground into a frenzy. But it was Saturday. The gates would be locked and there'd be no kids to play with.

Nope. The park was the obvious choice. Yet he wasn't here.

Oh no.

A terrible thought hit me. Perhaps he'd tried to come here and not made it. DaVinci's lifeless body might be lying invisible beside a road. No one would even know he was there until the flea collar batteries ran out and he became visible again. But by then, it would be too late.

I shook my head to get the image out of my mind.

"This is useless," I said to Granddad. "Should we walk back to the car and go for another drive?"

Granddad nodded sadly, his body stooped like one of the park lampposts.

As we strolled back along the path, nothing had changed.

The boy was no better at throwing his Frisbee, sending it rolling off along the ground in every direction except towards his poor dad.

The lady was still heaping food onto the four plates. Sandwiches, sausage rolls, chips. As I stared at the piles of food, my stomach growled. I hadn't eaten since breakfast.

I wanted to grab the closest one and shovel it into my mouth. But right then, I had bigger problems on my plate.

Hang on!

One of the plates on the picnic rug had much less food than the others. The lady noticed, too. She frowned and reached back into her wicker picnic basket, pulling out another two sausage rolls. She put them on the plate, then rummaged for something else. Her hand emerged with another sandwich, which she placed next to the … wait a minute … the sausage rolls were gone.

The lady froze, staring at the plate in confusion, her hand suspended above it.

She yelped.

The sandwich rose out of her hand, twisting and mushing up as it hovered just centimetres away from her fingers. It hung in mid-air for a few seconds, then moved downwards and

turned all mushy, while slowly fading away into thin air.

I froze, staring at the spot where the sandwich had been only seconds before.

The lady clambered backwards on her hands, knocking a paper cup over and spilling brown liquid on her picnic blanket. Her mouth hung open, and she took big panicky breaths.

"Oh. My. Gosh..." she said, still backing away, staring at the plates.

A sausage roll rose off one of the full plates, before bobbing away from her. It squished flat, fading into nothing.

DaVinci?

It had to be.

We'd found him!

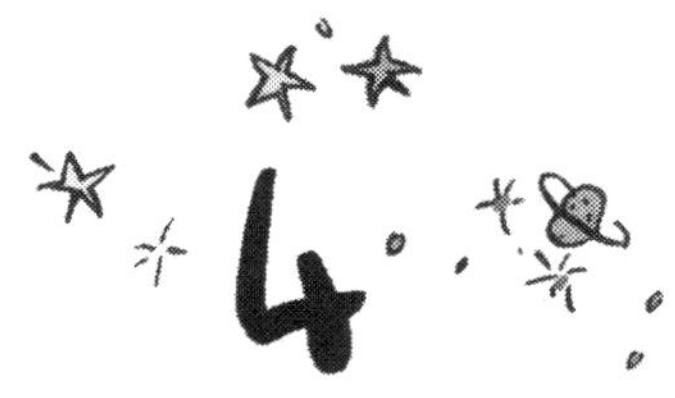

Far Fetched

I stared at the patch of grass beside the picnic rug, looking for clues. Surely DaVinci was there, unseen. Unless a sandwich-eating ghost was haunting the park.

Tugging at Granddad's shirt, I nodded towards the scene. The lady squatted on the far side of the chequered rug, her phone held at arm's length, pointing at the plates of food. She was breathing heavily, but otherwise could have been any old mum taking photos of her picnic.

Granddad shrugged.

I stared hard at the food, willing more of it to rise into the air. To reveal DaVinci's location.

Nothing happened.

Where was he? He couldn't have had enough to eat already. One time, DaVinci ate my entire eighth birthday cake, candles and all. There was no way a couple of sandwiches would fill him up.

Then I looked at the other picnickers nearby. Oh dear.

There was so much food.

Sausages.

Eggs.

Pies.

Pizza.

Fish and chips.

Even a pink unicorn birthday cake.

DaVinci could be anywhere. Eating anything.

An excited giggle tinkled behind me, followed by a gruff, "What the...?"

I spun around.

The small boy was chasing his Frisbee, arms outstretched, a huge smile on his face. But the Frisbee was hovering above the ground at a strange angle. Whenever the boy got close, the Frisbee bounded away from him.

I knew that game.

I'd played it with DaVinci a million times. In this very park.

I tugged at Granddad's shirt again and nodded towards the boy. His dad was jogging over to help.

When Granddad spotted the floating Frisbee, his eyes widened and he hobbled off to the right, circling around behind Invisi-Vinci.

I bent down with my arm outstretched, as I always did when I played fetch with DaVinci. Because he was great at the 'fetch' part, but terrible at the 'giving it back' part. You'd throw a ball or a Frisbee once, then spend the rest of the day trying to get it back off him.

"Give!" I said in my firmest voice.

The boy scowled at me. "Mine!" he said, stomping his foot.

"Oh, um, yes..." I forced a friendly smile. "I'll help you get it if you like?"

The Frisbee bounced up and down, jigging around in a strange pattern, like a bee doing its honey dance. DaVinci clearly thought I was here to play with him.

The boy glanced up at his dad, who stood beside him protectively. I smiled at him, too.

While I was distracted, the boy rushed forward, trying to grab the Frisbee by himself. It bounded off again, but Granddad had sneaked around behind DaVinci, his arms outstretched like a goalkeeper.

The Frisbee dropped to the ground.

Then Granddad fell backwards, sprawling out on the grass.

He let out an 'Oof!' and his shirt pressed into his stomach and chest. Granddad's arms shot up to protect his head, while his cheek and nose suddenly glistened.

I think DaVinci was standing on his chest, licking his face.

"Urgh, yuck!" Granddad spat.

Yes, the dog was definitely licking his face. And not for the first time. But you could normally see him coming, so it was easier to defend yourself.

Granddad's glistening hands now covered his nose and mouth.

The little boy stared wide-eyed, clutching his Frisbee to his chest. The dad gripped the boy's arm, dragging him away from the crazy old man.

I had to do something. Before DaVinci escaped again.

I rushed forward, my arms held wide, grasping at thin air. If I could just grab him, Granddad could get his collar off. Then the entire park would witness the world's best reappearing act. And everyone would realise that Granddad and I weren't barking mad.

Just as I reached Granddad, something soft squished underneath my foot.

DaVinci yelped, and I fell forward, landing elbows-first on Granddad's tummy.

He 'Oof'ed again.

"I'm sorry, I'm sorry!" I blurted, rolling off him. I reached out, hoping to grip fur, but only found thin air.

Oh no!

My clumsiness was the problem this time. But it was hardly my fault. Tripping over objects you can see is one thing ... but the dog was invisible. How was I supposed to know his tail or paw was right there?

Please let DaVinci be okay, I thought. I don't want to have injured him permanently.

I clambered up, then helped Granddad to his feet. Slowly. With lots of clicks coming from his knees and hips.

Once he was upright again, he dusted the grass off his clothes. "I'm too old for this!" he said with a grimace.

And I agreed with him.

I felt too old for it, too. And I was only eleven.

5. A Whole New Ball Game

I looked around the park. At the people filling the vast space. And the food laid out in front of them.

Was it me, or was everyone a bit quieter now? It felt like they all deliberately looked in the opposite direction when I glanced their way.

They had just seen me and Granddad tripping over thin air and rolling around on the ground with disgusted looks on our faces. If you didn't know there was invisible dog drool involved, you'd think we were weirdos!

"Maybe we should move along?" I said to Granddad under my breath. He nodded, and we headed towards the duck pond. No point going back to the car now that we knew DaVinci was in the park.

Somewhere.

Frisbee Boy and his dad had joined the lady on the picnic blanket, who now had four evenly distributed plates of food. An older girl was with them and they were all staring at the mum's phone, probably watching a video of disappearing food. At least, I hope that's what they were watching. If she'd recorded my and Granddad's slapstick performance, we might be about to go viral!

I glanced around nervously.

It was only a matter of time before DaVinci caused more havoc.

Sure enough, a scream rose from the middle of the park, followed by raised voices.

"Did you see that?"

"Oh, my days!"

"It just disappeared!"

My eyes focused on the commotion. A large group of picnickers with camping chairs and tables had all stood up and were staring at the ground, confused looks on their faces.

"My sausage!" a lady squealed. "It literally vanished!"

I broke into a jog, running straight for the crowd, though I had no idea what I'd do when I got there.

In the confusion, I slipped into their large circle unnoticed. I stared at a table piled high with bowls of chips and dips and meat. They'd even brought their own barbecue. No wonder DaVinci had headed here. It looked and smelled delicious.

But how was I supposed to know where he was? The food he ate only remained visible for a few seconds before it disappeared into his stomach. It was like trying to spot a sneeze in a snowstorm.

A scream sounded from elsewhere in the park.

DaVinci must have moved on already.

I smiled at a few of the picnickers, making my way out of the circle, jogging towards the sound of a girl crying.

What had DaVinci done now?

It didn't take long to figure that out.

The pink unicorn birthday cake had swapped its horn for two deep paw prints in the middle of its face.

Judging by the gaspy wails, the birthday girl wasn't too happy about it.

But where was DaVinci?

And Granddad, for that matter?

A shriek came from near the children's playground. A teenage boy lay on his back with a burger and fries spread across his chest.

He suddenly yelped and leapt to his feet, scattering his lunch on the ground.

"Eww! What was that?" he squealed, as his friends looked on, laughing. "It felt like something licked me!"

I glimpsed Granddad running towards the scene. Or limping, rather. He weaved through the teenagers, and when he got to the unhappy Happy Meal spread on the grass, he held his arms out, scanning the area in front of him like he was blindfolded.

Another scream came from the next group of people over.

Oh no. DaVinci had moved on already.

I started to jog in that direction, then stopped myself.

This was no good. We'd never find DaVinci like this. He was always one step ahead of us.

Instead of going to him, we needed to make DaVinci come to us.

I turned and walked towards the clearing beside the duck pond, where there were fewer people. As I went, I took the backpack off and rummaged inside.

The doggy treats would be no use here, as all the picnic blankets and tables were piled high with much yummier food. The lead was also useless until we caught him. But the bald tennis ball? That could work.

The muddy bank beside the duck pond was clear, except for the toddler and her grandma, who seemed to have a never-ending supply of bread to feed the ducks.

I ignored them, took a deep breath, and shouted "Here boy!" in my most playful dog-owner voice.

Nothing happened, so I bounced the tennis ball at my feet and caught it.

"Come on, DaVinci, you good boy! Come play with Fingers."

I could sense people looking at me, but this was no time to be self-conscious. And anyway, they'd assume I was calling my normal, obedient, visible dog. Rather than DaVinci, who was none of those things.

Granddad was hobbling towards me, hunched over with one hand pressed against his lower back. He must have hurt himself when he fell. And realised that chasing an invisible dog was futile.

I bounced the ball at my feet again.

And again.

"Come on, boy! Finn's got a ballie!"

A galloping sound filled my ears. Paws hitting the ground, getting closer by the second.

Granddad sped up, glancing behind him.

Then his feet lifted into the air and he crashed down onto his back with a thud.

Ouch.

Poor Granddad.

DaVinci had a habit of running at people's legs, but you could usually see him coming and dodge out of the way.

The galloping got louder again.

I braced myself for impact, clutching the ball to my stomach.

Oof!

A force hit me right between the legs, doubling me over.

I fell forward, still clutching the ball, my face crashing straight into the muddy ground, rattling my brain.

A wet slobbery tongue wormed its way between my fingers, trying to get at the ball.

Then, ow!

Teeth.

DaVinci chomped the ball, trying to get it off me.

This was his favourite game.

It was usually one of my favourites, too. But that was when I could see his teeth. I gripped the ball with both hands, only using the thumb and index finger of each, leaving enough space for DaVinci's teeth.

The ball squished between my fingers as the dog clamped down on it.

I wasn't going to let go, though. No way.

Lying on the muddy bank with my arms outstretched, I held on for dear life. My stomach scraped the ground as DaVinci actually pulled me along.

Where the heck was Granddad? I couldn't hold on for much longer.

DaVinci's grip went slack for a second, then pain exploded in my left thumb.

Ow, ow, ow!

I let go of the ball with one hand, clutching it to my stomach, gritting my teeth against the pain.

DaVinci had just done that thing where he chomps forward to get a better grip and caught my finger in the process.

Heavy footfalls and huffing announced Granddad's arrival. I only had to hold on for a few more seconds.

I could do this.

No, no, no...

The ball slipped from my grasp, jerking back in mid-air towards the pond.

Granddad squatted beside me, arms spread wide. I leapt to my feet and did the same.

The ball hovered by the muddy bank, a string of saliva hanging from it like an icicle.

We had him pinned between us and the pond.

6. Like a Duck to Water

I ducked low and closed in. Granddad did the same. We wouldn't let DaVinci get away this time.

I glanced to my right. The old lady stood beside the pond, shielding her granddaughter from us. She must have witnessed my getting-dragged-along-the-ground-by-nothing trick and was worried what stunt I'd pull next.

The little girl was oblivious. She just reached her hand into the bag and pulled out half a slice of white bread.

I wanted to scream, "Don't do it!"

But the only sound was the ducks honking with excitement and flapping their wings to get to the front of the flock.

The girl swung her entire arm around, like she was bowling a cricket ball, and threw it into the pond.

The slice of bread fell rather than flew. It flopped into the muddy water only a metre from the bank, causing a frenzy of quacks and flapping wings.

In front of me and Granddad, the floating ball dropped out of the air. It squelched onto the mud and rolled towards the water's edge, followed by a trail of saliva.

I braced myself for what I knew was coming.

SPLASH!

Water sprayed up in a line, heading straight for the ducky commotion.

The birds all quacked at once and flew into the air, escaping the unseen predator.

All except one of them.

The lucky ducky that had reached the chunk of bread first suddenly wasn't so lucky.

As its flock dispersed, the poor duck flapped just as hard, but didn't go anywhere.

Its butt rose up, but its head seemed clamped in place, the bread still in its beak.

DaVinci had the poor thing's neck in his teeth!

I could tell because droplets of water dappled his fur, creating a ghostly effect.

Beside us, the old lady shrieked and the little girl said, "Look, Nanna, a ghost doggie!"

The chunk of bread separated from the duck's beak, squishing and morphing as it moved down DaVinci's throat and slowly disappeared.

Having swallowed the bread, DaVinci opened his ghostly mouth and the duck shot into the air, its flapping finally propelling it away.

Ghost-Vinci bounded out of the water in big splashy strides until he reached the bank between us and the terrified old lady. Thousands of tiny droplets of water shimmered on his fur, outlining him perfectly. But we could still see the pond through him.

He really did look like a phantom.

"We need to catch him now!" I blurted, knowing what was coming next.

Sure enough, DaVinci shook himself, spraying me, Granddad, the old lady, and her granddaughter with a fine mist of pond water. I wiped my face on my sleeve, and when I looked back, DaVinci was barely visible. There was a second shuddering sound, followed by another light spray, and DaVinci disappeared before my eyes.

I dropped to the arms-out-squat position, my eyes trained on the exact spot where he'd disappeared. But nothing was there.

He had completely vanished.

Again.

Then a wet paw print appeared on the ground in front of me. And another. As he stepped forward, he left a trail of wet prints behind him. But they wouldn't last long. We had to catch him right now.

I leapt at the space above the two most recent prints in a flying rugby tackle, my arms outstretched. My left hand brushed something waggy. My face rammed into damp fur.

And the smell.

Eww, no.

I'd hit the wrong end!

Frankly, I'd preferred the teeth to this. But I gripped fur with both hands, as the lower half of my body slammed into the ground at the edge of the pond.

DaVinci yapped playfully and tried to pull away, but I held firm.

I also held my breath.

Wet fur slapped one cheek. Then the other. And back again.

Yuck.

Yuck.

Yuck.

Grimacing, I locked my mouth shut as DaVinci's tail continued to slap me about the face, my nose only centimetres from his bum.

"Help me, Granddad," I shouted. Although, what actually came out was, "Hmph mm, grrnaa!"

Fortunately, Granddad got the message, rushing around in front of me as I held desperately on to DaVinci's rear, smelly tail-wags swiping my face from side to side.

The problem is, Granddad came in too hard and fast. He must have thought I was gripping the dog side on, rather than by the stinky end.

There was a dreadful crunch, which sounded like Granddad's knee connecting with DaVinci's head, then Granddad tumbled forward. He put his hands out to break the fall, but the bank dipped away, and he shot over the edge. Granddad's hands squelched into the mud at the edge of the pond. Followed closely by his face.

I could see it all happening in slow motion through DaVinci's body, despite the fact that my clenched face was still pressing into his butt.

The tail slapping increased. DaVinci thought we were playing with him.

But the smell was too much and I released my grip, rolling onto my side and taking huge lungfuls of clean, dog-butt-free air.

Granddad rose from the pond like a monster emerging from the deep, his arms and face covered in thick black mud.

It would have been hilarious if we hadn't just lost the dog again.

I looked away from Granddad, out towards the picnic area, which had gone eerily quiet. Mums, dads, kids, and teenagers all stared our way, eyes wide.

Granddad stood still, as though frozen by their gaze.

I stared hard at the ground in front of me, my face flushing with warmth.

The only signs that DaVinci had been there were a few faint footprints, Granddad's coating of mud and my blushing face.

I closed my eyes and wished it was me that was invisible, not that stupid dog.

Clear as Mud

I stared at the muddy ground. Four wet paw prints darkened the mud in front of me, then trailed off to the right along the edge of the pond, getting gradually fainter.

"We need to follow him!" I said, glancing up at Granddad. "Before the prints ... fade." I trailed off.

The whites of Granddad's eyes were glistening in a mask of black mud. It covered his hair, his face, his arms, and his chest. In fact, his whole top half was coated, as though he'd been dangled by the ankles and dipped into a vat of dark chocolate.

He gazed through me, as if I too had turned invisible.

I waved a hand in front of his face, but Granddad's expression didn't change. Perhaps it couldn't. The mud might be so thick that he'd be stuck like that until we could wash it off.

Or maybe he didn't want to risk opening his mouth, in case some mud slipped in.

Come to think of it, it smelled pretty bad from a couple of metres away. Perhaps the stench had overpowered him? Sent him into a stupor?

I glanced at the paw prints on the ground, which were now barely visible. Uh-oh. There was no time to waste. I quickly led Granddad to a nearby bench, placing my hand on his hip, below the mud line.

"Sit here, Granddad."

He plonked onto his bottom and stared out over the pond, looking half like those buskers who paint themselves like statues on street corners. Perhaps I should put a hat down to collect money? Or half a hat?

On second thoughts, he smelled so bad no one would want to come near him.

"Don't go anywhere," I said gently. "I'll be back in a minute."

His expression remained unchanged. In fact, he didn't even blink. Like a proper statue.

I spun on my heel and jogged after the paw prints. They followed the bank of the pond to the path. Then they stopped. I looked left. And right.

Nothing.

DaVinci had vanished.

But I guess I already knew that.

Then I spotted a smear of dark mud on a leaf. The woods were generally impenetrable, but the undergrowth here had been trampled into a faint opening. Maybe DaVinci went in there?

I glanced around the park. No one was staring at me or Granddad any more. They'd gone back to chatting, eating, playing football... all the normal Saturday-in-the-park activities.

And there were no signs of disappearing sandwiches or sniffed bottoms. Perhaps DaVinci was in the woods?

I cut across the path and pushed the undergrowth aside. It parted easily, like a hidden entranceway. When my eyes adjusted to the gloom, I saw a rough path through the trees leading to a clearing. I clambered through, rustling leaves and snapping twigs underfoot. If DaVinci was in here, he'd definitely hear me coming.

A gruff sound came from up ahead.

"Wha-huh?"

Was that animal or human? Surely it had to be DaVinci. No one else would hide in here on such a nice day, would they?

"Hello?" I called.

No response.

I ploughed my way through the undergrowth, trying to step carefully.

I failed.

My left foot twisted on a knobbly stick or a rock, and I fell forward, stumbling into the clearing and landing on my hands and knees.

At that moment, something warm and wet pressed into my cheek, and a waft of dog breath filled my nostrils.

DaVinci.

It had to be.

Unless there was an invisible rubbish bin with a wet nose hiding in this clearing.

I knelt, reaching out and stroking thin air a few times, until my hand encountered damp fur. Then I continued stroking him and scratching behind an ear that I could feel but not see.

"Hello, boy," I said, scratching harder as he pushed into me. With the other hand, I felt my way along to DaVinci's neck, and gripped the collar, which vibrated steadily between my fingers.

"Gotcha!"

No way was I letting go this time.

My fingers found a buckle at the bottom of the thick collar. Gripping it tightly with one hand, I fumbled with it until it popped open.

The collar instantly appeared in my hand, as if by magic.

I stared at the empty space in front of me. Slowly, like a Polaroid photo developing before my eyes, DaVinci came into focus.

A gasp came from the other side of the clearing. Woah!

What I'd thought was a bundle of clothes had a person in it. A man with a bushy beard and wide eyes. Eyes that were staring hard at DaVinci. No... wait. He was looking at me.

"Eet's you!" the man said, and my mouth dropped open. I'd recognise that voice anywhere!

It was Jesus. The short security guard from the hospital. The one I once swapped bodies with.

What the heck was he doing here?

Pointing Fingers

Jesus backed away from me, leaving a trail of dirty blankets.

His eyes bored into mine.

"Eet's you!" he repeated. "Dios mio!"

"Jesus!" I said, the word scraping on my dry throat.

His expression crackled with what ... anger? "You say eet Hey-ZEUS!"

He glanced around as if looking for an escape route.

Hang on... it wasn't anger. It was fear. He was scared. Of me.

He'd just witnessed a dog appear before his very eyes, yet it was me that scared him.

"It's okay," I said, holding my hands out, palms down. The collar dangled from my left hand, jingling slightly.

DaVinci sniffed at one of the blankets, then whined faintly. I didn't blame him. I could smell them from here. A cheesy, old-shoe smell that singed my nostril hair.

"Leave me alone!" Jesus said, cowering away from me.

"What...? Why...?" I couldn't find the rest of the words. This was just too strange. Jesus, the short but proud security guard who patrolled the hospital like a watchdog. Who figured out that Granddad had swapped bodies with a dog. Who helped me fix the whole mind-swapping mess!

What was he doing living in a clearing in the woods? Smelling like a three-day-old lunchbox? It didn't make sense.

Then Jesus's frown darkened further, the dirty skin surrounding his beard forming deep furrows.

"Ees your fault!" he said, firing his words at me from the other side of the clearing. "All thees!"

He gestured at the trees, the blankets, the bed of newspapers that he'd been sleeping on.

My jaw dropped open. "But..."

What did he mean this was my fault? How could I have anything to do with him living rough in the woods? I'm just a kid.

"Ze first time, they think I crazy. They watch me. Then with ze robot... They say eet too dangerous. I endanger old lady and child. I lose my job. Then I no pay my rent."

I stared at him, blinking. My eyes drawn to yellow smear on his beard that looked like egg yolk.

It's...

But...

Me?

It can't be my fault, can it? Okay, so I used the mind-swapper on him so he could help me carry it out of the hospital. And yes, I did boss a few people around while in his body.

Endangering an old lady?

Okay, yes. It was my fault that Mrs Taylor was in hospital, and I leapt the robo-dog over her to get back to my own body.

But I went nowhere near any children.

Unless...

...I was the child!

The hospital had fired Jesus after he let a dangerous machine into the building. And I was that machine. But from their viewpoint, a crazed robo-dog had endangered Mrs Taylor and me - Finn Butterby. They had no idea it was me trying to get things back to normal!

It really was my fault that Jesus got fired.

And that he was sleeping rough in the park.

I... I couldn't believe it.

I've always been pretty good at messing things up. Heck, I hospitalised my entire family in a single day. But this? This was a whole new level. I'd literally ruined someone's life.

The hatred in his eyes shrivelled my heart to the size of a raisin. I lowered my gaze, not wanting to look at him. At his dirty clothes and face and beard. I wished I could avert my nose, too, but the smell was still there. A lingering reminder, no matter where I looked.

DaVinci snuffled at the ground, sniffing a leaf.

Chatter and laughter drifted over from the picnics.

And yet here was Jesus, hiding in the woods.

Nowhere to go.

No money.

No roof over his head.

All because of me.

I had to do something. But what? What could I possibly do to get Jesus his job back? Or to pay his rent? I barely had enough pocket money to buy lollies.

I glanced at the dog collar in my hand. Mmmm. It had turned DaVinci invisible. There had to be value in that. What if it worked on humans, too? Surely people would pay a lot to be invisible. Perhaps I could use it to raise funds for Jesus?

But what would Granddad say about that?

Oh no... Granddad!

I'd left him sitting on the bench next to the pond.

"I've got to go!" I said, backing out of the clearing. "But... I'll..."

I wanted to say, "I'll help you!" or "I'll be back!" but judging by the look on Jesus's face, those were the last things he wanted to hear from me, so I just backed away.

I needed to get out of there. To breathe some fresh air and clear my head.

To come up with a plan to help Jesus get his life back.

Duck Away

Stepping out of the undergrowth onto the path was like being reborn. The sunlight and fresh air felt new and different. Like I'd never experienced them properly before.

I felt different, too.

I'd only been in the woods for a moment, yet my whole world had changed.

Because I'd changed someone's whole world.

And I knew who had to fix the mess I'd made.

Me.

Fingers Butterby.

I glanced over at the pond. Granddad sat on the bench, completely unmoved. Several ducks pecked at the ground by his feet.

Just as I stepped towards him, my legs were swept from underneath me, flying up into the air behind a blur of fur.

I thumped onto my back and DaVinci twirled round and licked my mouth, wafting his smelly pants right up my nose.

Eww.

The delightful aroma of fishy dog breath.

It beat Jesus's cheesy shoe stench, but not by much.

I grabbed DaVinci in a bear hug, pulling him off his feet and onto the ground beside me. I didn't want him running away, even when I could see him.

The problem was, I still had his collar in my hand. And I couldn't risk putting it back on him. Keeping a handful of fur, I slipped my bag off my shoulder and edged the zip open with one hand. I shoved the invisibility collar into the bag and pulled out the lead.

With DaVinci not wearing a collar, I had to loop the lead around itself and put the noose round DaVinci's neck. I was slightly worried that he might strangle himself, as he's not clever enough to know when to stop pulling. But it would be hard enough getting Granddad back to the car without having to chase after DaVinci again.

I clambered to my feet and let DaVinci drag me over towards the bench. His tongue lolled to the side and I'm sure his skin was turning blue, yet it didn't slow him down.

The ducks scattered at our approach, and Granddad didn't even flinch.

Oh no.

I hadn't broken him, too, had I?

Please let him be okay after a warm shower.

The mud covering his top half had dried like cement. Could he even move? It was pretty thick.

"Granddad?" I said softly. "Are you okay?"

He shuddered, then his head turned to face me, the mud on his neck cracking and flaking off in places.

His eyes stared right through me.

"Look... I've got DaVinci. We can go home now!"

Nothing.

"Come on," I said, grabbing his arm and dragging him onto his feet. "Up you get."

The mud cracked and scraped my fingers, but Granddad came willingly, if slowly.

With DaVinci pulling me along by one arm and Granddad holding me back with the other, it felt like I might split in two.

We made our way down the path. The lady with the picnic eyed us suspiciously and the boy who'd been playing Frisbee pointed and said something to his dad.

Yet no one stopped us. Or ran away screaming.

When we got to Granddad's car, I questioned the wisdom of letting him drive us home. But he seemed to switch into autopilot mode as soon as he got the keys out. I opened the boot for DaVinci, then jumped into the passenger seat and Granddad drove us towards home without hitting anything or causing any accidents, which was the most luck we'd had all day.

"Can you drop me at our place?" I asked as we approached the turnoff. Granddad grunted and flicked the indicator. This was going pretty well, all things considered.

As Granddad pulled up outside my house, I thought about mentioning the invisibility collar in my bag. But it might come in handy. Surely he wouldn't miss it for a day or two. He should probably have a break from inventing, anyway. Put his feet up.

I slammed the car door and stared at DaVinci. His slobbery face pressed against the back window, surrounded by smears of dribble.

Granddad didn't pull away. He just stared straight ahead, as though he'd forgotten what he was supposed to be doing.

DaVinci barked and bashed his nose against the window, as if he wanted to come with me.

The thing is ... would Granddad even be able to look after the dog in this state? Probably not. What if he escaped again? Would that be my fault, too?

No.

I couldn't let that happen.

"Hey, Granddad," I said, slowly opening the car door so I didn't startle him. "Should I look after DaVinci for the day? Bring him back this evening once you've cleaned up and are feeling better?"

"Mmm," he said, nodding. "What a splendid idea."

I wasn't sure he'd actually registered what I said, but that was all the encouragement I needed. I opened the back door and DaVinci leapt out, jumping up at me and licking my face. He clearly thought it would be more fun spending the day with me than with a comatose Granddad.

I gave Granddad a friendly wave, then watched as he pootled off down the street. At the crossroads he turned in the right direction, which was a good sign.

As I used my key to let us in, DaVinci jumped up at me, leaving brown paw prints on my T-shirt.

"Hi, Mum. Hi, Dad," I said, as DaVinci ran circles around me. "We've got a visitor for the afternoon!"

Mum and Dad both groaned, but they were mostly joking. We'd looked after DaVinci a lot recently, since Mum was warming to the idea of getting a dog. She'd even bought him food and water bowls, saying we might need them for our own dog one day. Right now, she filled both bowls and placed them by the back door.

DaVinci sniffed the food, then turned away and lapped at the water. Wow … he's never turned down food before. He must have eaten even more than I thought at the picnic.

The picnic!

That reminded me. About Jesus. And the invisibility collar.

"Sorry, Mum … stuff to do," I said, rushing up the stairs, three at a time.

I burst into Sally's room without knocking.

She wasn't there.

Blast it.

Where was she?

I needed her help to figure out what I could do about Jesus.

In the meantime, I pulled the invisibility collar out of my bag, turning it over in my hands. Maybe I could figure this out instead. I might as well have some fun while I waited for Sally to get home.

See for Yourself

I stood in front of the mirror in my bedroom, the flea collar held in my hands, vibrating like the dryer when it's on full spin.

Could this really work? On humans?

There was only one way to find out.

I looped it around my neck, tightened it, and threaded the buckle through.

The vibrations jiggled my throat and my Adam's apple, then spread out to my chest and face. My teeth chattered, like on a cold morning.

Then the vibrations reached my ears, the top of my head, my tummy. They rushed down my arms, making my fingers tingle, and continued all the way to the tips of my toes.

But I was still visible. I could see myself twitching and vibrating. Even my hair quivered.

My vision blurred, because my eyeballs were shaking in their sockets.

I closed my eyes and massaged them with my fingertips.

The Batman picture on my T-shirt looked like it was vibrating, too.

Wait a minute.

My eyes were closed with my hands covering them. How could I still see my Batman T-shirt?

I turned and looked around the room. I could feel my eyes shut, my fingertips pressing into them. Yet I could see my bed, my Arsenal poster, the window. And it was really bright.

I looked back at the mirror.

No way!

My T-shirt hung in mid-air, directly above my jeans. It was inflated like a balloon, but I could see down through the neck hole to the label at

ARSENAL
AFC
NBA

the back. The letter 'M' and the washing instructions were all in mirror image.

I held my hands a few inches from my face, waving them around.

Nothing.

Absolutely nothing.

Just empty air before my eyes.

Woah! This was so cool!

Think of all the pranks I could pull.

It would be hilarious!

I wanted to rush downstairs to show Mum and Dad, but they would totally freak out if only my clothes walked into the room. And then what would they do? Surely they'd make me take the collar off and give it back to Granddad.

No way.

I needed this collar. It could help me help Jesus.

Instead, I slipped the T-shirt over my head, enjoying the brief lack of brightness.

Then I held it at arm's length, waving it around before flinging it onto my bed.

It was like the best magic trick ever.

I walked around my room, watching my jeans in the mirror. A pair of ghost legs strolling along.

I slipped my jeans off, dangling them at head height for a moment before flinging them in a wide arc onto my bed.

All I could see in the mirror now were my red undies and my socks, one green one blue. I never could be bothered finding matching pairs.

I took off the green one first. Then the blue. I did a funny little sock dance in front of the mirror before chucking them on the floor.

Then I looked down at my undies.

It was so weird seeing the inside of them like that.

Should I?

I hesitated.

The only way to be completely invisible was to take them off. But then I'd be naked.

What if the collar ran out of batteries while I was creeping around the house? It could happen in front of Mum or Dad. Or Sally. How embarrassing would that be?

But it was worth the risk.

I slipped my undies off and kicked them up into the air. They missed my bed, landing on top of my bedside lamp.

Now the mirror showed absolutely nothing.

Wow... Granddad was an utter genius. Even if this wasn't intentional. He'd created a collar that could turn anyone invisible.

Okay, so that person had to be stark naked, but still.

This was brilliant.

My bedroom door opened, as though by magic, and I stepped out onto the landing. It was even brighter out here. I squinted out of habit, but it did nothing to block the light, so I relaxed my face and crept down the stairs.

Even avoiding the creaky third step, they made way too much noise. I placed my foot down as gently as possible, but the wood creaked and a perfect footprint appeared on the carpet below me. My breath wheezed in and out through my nose.

If someone was standing right next to me, surely they'd know I was here?

It took a full minute to get down the stairs in stealth mode. And I think stealth mode might have looked like a nude version of the Scoobie-Doo tiptoe pose. But fortunately, no one could see me.

I was invisible.

And it was time to make the most of it.

Unbelievable Behaviour

I tiptoed into the kitchen, breathing through my mouth so I didn't make a sound.

Mum and Dad sat at the dining table, their half-eaten lunches in front of them. Dad had the newspaper in his hand and Mum was staring at her phone.

Fortunately, DaVinci was asleep on a blanket in the corner. His invisible mischief in the park must have worn him out.

I stood there for a moment, feeling the breeze from the open window in places that don't normally feel the breeze.

What should I even do?

I hadn't thought further ahead than testing out my powers. Perhaps pulling a few pranks. But now I was there, I wasn't feeling very inspired. In fact, I felt a bit like a fart. Present, but unseen and unwelcome.

Come on, brain, I thought. I've dreamt of moments like this.

Okay.

Start small.

I leaned forward, stretched my arm out, and tweaked the corner of the newspaper.

Dad's eyes flicked towards the open window, then back at his article. He absentmindedly plucked a cherry tomato from the salad in front of him and popped it in his mouth.

I flicked the paper again. Harder this time.

"It's quite windy today," Dad said.

'Mmm,' said Mum in response.

Why wasn't he reacting more? Surely he should be freaking out by now.

I grabbed the corner of the newspaper and yanked it hard.

Dad's eyes narrowed, but he just pushed his plate aside and laid the newspaper down on the table.

Okay, I clearly needed to step things up a notch.

Still reading, Dad reached his arm out to grab the last tomato off its nest of lettuce. Just before he got it, I flicked it across the bowl. Dad's fingers pinched at thin air and he glanced over. His eyes went back to his newspaper and his fingers moved towards the tomato's new location.

I gave it another flick.

When his fingers pinched thin air again, Dad frowned and stared hard at the tomato. Without taking his eyes off it, he crept his hand forward, like a cat approaching a mouse.

I grabbed the tomato and lifted it about ten centimetres off the plate. Dad's eyes followed, intense, but not exactly freaked out. His fingers darted forward, plucking it out of the air. His skin glanced against mine, and I held my breath, expecting … what? I don't know. Some sort of reaction, at least.

All he did was pop the tomato in his mouth and look back at the newspaper.

I grabbed a handful of lettuce and lifted it into the air, but Dad kept his eyes on the article he was reading.

This was not going as planned.

Okay ... maybe I should try Mum instead. She's always quicker to react.

I dropped the lettuce and crept around to Mum's side of the table.

It was so weird being this close to them without being noticed. How could they not hear me? My heart thumping in my chest was even louder than my footfalls.

But Mum's eyes stayed glued to her phone as she took a bite of her sandwich and dropped the crust onto her plate.

Unfair! She always makes me eat the crust, then doesn't do it herself!

Never mind ... it gave me something to play with.

I picked the crust off her plate, hovering it in mid-air.

Mum glanced at it, then back at her phone.

What was wrong with these people?

I held it a metre off the table and swung it from side to side.

Jeez. Still nothing.

I took a few steps into the kitchen and waved the crust in wide circles like I was about to fling it to the ducks.

Mum glanced at it, massaged both temples with her thumbs and forefingers, then looked back at her phone. "My concussion's still really bad," she said.

"Me too," said Dad, looking up at the incredible flying crust. He blinked a few times and rubbed his eyes. "You'd think it'd be better by now. It's been months since the accidents."

My heart started beating even louder.

The accidents. When I knocked both my parents out and hospitalised them.

That's what this was about? That was why they weren't fazed by flying food?

They were blaming their head injuries.

Injuries that I caused.

My arms flopped to my sides.

Not only had I made Jesus homeless, I'd also broken my parents to the point where they didn't even believe their own eyes.

My actions caused all this. Did all this damage. Me.

Suddenly, pain exploded in my fingers.

"Arrgh!" I yelped, staring down at my hand only to see DaVinci's mouth clamped around the crust. And my invisible fingers!

DaVinci bit down again and I clamped my other hand over my mouth to stop myself from screaming.

I tried to pull away, but DaVinci locked his legs into tug-of-war mode. He wasn't letting free food go, even after his picnics in the park.

Relaxing my fingers, I let go of the bread. DaVinci's tongue wriggled as he swallowed the crust whole. With the food devoured, DaVinci opened his mouth, and I snatched my fingers back, gently massaging them with my other hand.

"Get back in your basket," Dad said, without looking up. "There's a good boy."

DaVinci didn't get back in his basket. His nose twitched and stretched forward, his tail wagging.

Oh no.

He'd picked up my scent.

I turned and bolted, but not quickly enough. A wet, cold dog's nose pressed right into my bum.

"Eeeeooooow!" I squeaked, spinning around. Better to deal with DaVinci head on. At least I could see him coming.

The dog leapt at me, his paws appearing to stop in mid-air as they dug into my stomach.

His tongue licked my lips and nose and eyeball, and I squished my face as closed as it would go.

"Wow ... look what the dog can do now!" Mum said, and they stared at me. Or at the dog, who was standing on his hind legs in the middle of the kitchen.

"I didn't think you could teach an old dog new tricks. Not that dog, anyway."

I backed away slowly and DaVinci followed me, walking across the room on two legs.

"The kids must have taught him," Dad said. "Impressive." His attention returned to the newspaper.

I grimaced as DaVinci's claws dug deeper into my stomach, then he licked my mouth again, his tongue sliding over my teeth.

My back thumped into the shelves, and a family photo toppled over.

"Don't break anything, you daft dog,' Mum said, looking up at DaVinci whose front half appeared to be hovering thirty centimetres from the shelf. Then her eyes returned to her phone.

Clearly nothing would faze her today.

DaVinci licked my eyeball and I tried to push him away, but that made him more excited. He yapped in my face, his doggy breath going straight up my nostrils.

I was trapped in the kitchen by an overexcited dog.

The only positive was that it didn't seem to matter what we did. My parents probably wouldn't bat an eyelid if DaVinci started juggling kitchen knives. They'd just blame their concussion and carry on as they were.

But how could I get out of there?

Keys jangled at the front door and DaVinci's ears twitched.

Sally!

She must have just got home.

DaVinci pushed off, giving me one final scratch on the stomach, and rushed to the front door.

That was my cue to get the heck out of there.

I took the stairs three at a time, the sound of my footsteps drowned out by Sally getting mauled by the dog.

Phew. I'd escaped.

But that was a complete fail.

Let's hope I have more success pranking Sally.

Listen, Sister

I ducked into Sally's room, and stood on the other side of the bed, where she wouldn't see my footprints in the carpet.

What should I do to announce myself?

In the past, I'd have kept the invisibility secret from her as long as possible, using it to drive her totally bonkers. But not any more. We'd been getting on pretty well recently. And I needed her help to figure out what to do about Jesus.

But I was invisible.

I had to have a little fun first.

I glanced around her room.

Her skanky old teddy, Marvin, sat on her pillow. Maybe I could animate him? Make him stand up and stroll along the edge of the bed.

That would totally freak her out.

And there was all her makeup on the dresser. What if one of her lipsticks hovered in the air, then wrote something on the mirror?

Perhaps, "Mirror, mirror on the wall ... who's the fartiest of them all?"

Or something creepy, like "You're not alone!"

The thing is, what if she freaked out too much? She might keel over and hurt herself. Or die of fright.

Or what if she didn't freak out? Like Mum and Dad. She might talk to Marvin, as though that was normal. Or ignore the writing and carry on staring at her phone.

After all, she'd had the worst concussion out of anybody. All because I rode a skateboard down the highway in her body. Without wearing a helmet. And I crashed so badly she saw double for a month.

I flopped onto Sally's bed with my head in my hands.

Suddenly, doing nothing seemed like the best idea.

At least that way, nobody would get hurt. I wouldn't cause any more homelessness or break anyone else's mind.

Right at that moment, I didn't want to do anything ever again. It wasn't worth the consequences.

Then the door flung open and my sister walked in, looking around. "Fingers, are you in here?"

My eyes widened.

Sally must have been to the hairdressers. Instead of her normal droopy blond hair, she had … what?

Style.

I barely recognised her. Her head was shaved down one side but shoulder length on the other. And she looked funky. Like a rock star. Especially with the nose piercing she'd got last week.

Even this new cool Sally was probably my fault. The boring old Sally wouldn't never have dreamt of standing out like that.

"Weird!" she said after scanning the room and finding it empty. Then she turned and bounded off down the stairs.

I got up and ambled back to my bedroom, my head hung low.

Who knows how long I sat there, staring at the wall? I'd somehow put my clothes on and the invisibility collar lay on my desk, not fulfilling its potential.

All my enthusiasm had vanished.

Jesus was out there, both looking and sleeping rough.

Mum and Dad had stopped believing what they saw, no matter how crazy it was.

And Sally... She had clearly changed, too.

Because of me. It was all my fault.

Seriously.

Everything I touch turns to muck. Like the opposite of the Midas touch, where instead of gold, things turn into poo.

A knock startled me from my thoughts, and Sally's head poked around the edge of the door.

"There you are!" she said, smiling. "Wassup?"

I tried to return the smile, but the corners of my mouth had a long way to climb. They made it as far as horizontal. Definitely not a smile.

"Jeez. Why so glum?" Sally asked, waltzing into my room. "It's the weekend, yet you look like you're in a Monday-morning maths test."

I shrug.

"And do you like my hair?" she asked, striking a pose.

I nodded, but still couldn't conjure up a smile.

Sally perched on the edge of my bed and nudged me. "Go on. Spill the beans."

Sometimes I think I preferred it when Sally was the one in a bad mood.

I took a deep breath and tried to start at the beginning.

"Granddad's new collar doesn't just get rid of fleas. It turns the wearer invisible and ..."

"Hang on!" Sally said, holding both palms out like she was directing traffic. "You're telling me ... Granddad has invented an invisibility collar ... and you're sad about it? Why aren't you out there moving road signs or sneaking into the cinema?"

I bit my lip. "DaVinci was invisible, and he led me into a clearing and I saw Jesus."

"Wow. You had an epiphany. Were angels singing?"

"What, no! Not that Jesus. The security guard. From the hospital."

"Oh, Hey-ZEUS, right." Sally nodded. "Was he as happy as ever?"

"Well, no, I mean, yes. He … he … lost his job."

"Oh, that's a shame. He seemed to really enjoy it." Sally smirked.

She wasn't getting it. "But he lost it because of me. He was on probation after we swapped bodies. Then the robo-dog was the final straw. Now he's living on the street because he couldn't pay his rent. And Mum and Dad aren't right either. I tried pranking them, but they didn't believe their own eyes. They just blamed their … their accidents.."

I used a sniffly sob as an exclamation mark.

Then Sally hugged me … and the sobs wouldn't stop coming. I kept thinking about Jesus, and Mum and Dad, and Granddad, and all the other damage I'd caused.

"Hey, it's not your fault. These things happen." She rubbed my back, which made me sob even louder. "And anyway … I was there, too. We're in this together."

She was all right, my sister.

I sat up and dried my eyes on my sleeves. Then I glanced at the invisibility collar.

"Ooh, is that it?" Sally said, picking it up and turning it round in her hands.

I nodded. "I thought we might use it to get Jesus's job back. The one problem is, the invisibility only works if you're naked."

Sally snorted with laughter.

"What, so one of us needs to stroll into the hospital in the nude? Dibs not me!"

I hung my head and sniffed.

"No, wait. You're right. There must be something we can do. Invisibility is like a superpower. And with the skin-tight outfits most superheroes wear, they might as well be naked. What were you thinking?"

That was the problem. I hadn't been thinking. And I didn't want to think. All my ideas turned into utter disasters and ruined people's lives.

I shrugged.

"Alright, so what do we know?"

"That Jesus lost his job and is now living on the street."

"Yes, and we know how he lost it. We just don't know how he can get it back. Or if he'd even want it back. He wasn't exactly Mr Happy-Employee-of-the-Month."

"If you thought he was grumpy before, you should see him now."

"Maybe we should go visit him," Sally said. "Let's take him some food and drink, see if that gets him talking."

The corners of my mouth rose into an almost-smile. I knew Sally would know what to do.

She gave my shoulder a gentle squeeze and gestured to the door.

Half an hour later we were on our bikes, heading towards the park. Our stomachs and Sally's basket were filled with ham-and-cheese sandwiches. The sun was shining, and we had the beginnings of a plan. We'd talk to Jesus and figure out what we could do to help.

13

Gone to the Dogs

"He's through here," I said, pointing at the slight gap in the undergrowth beside the path.

Sally raised her eyebrows towards the blue sky, as though she didn't believe me. But she dismounted anyway and laid her bike on the grass, pulling Jesus's packed lunch out of the basket.

I laid my bike on top of Sally's, hoping the prospect of disentangling them would be enough to deter any thieves.

Then I ducked through the gap and into the gloom, spurred on by Sally crashing along behind me.

When I stepped out into the clearing, it was ... well ... clear. There were no clothes or blankets. No signs of Jesus at all. It was like he had vanished.

Sally joined me in surveying the area. "Maybe you did have an epiphany, after all."

"But ... he was here," I said, staring at the flattened patch of ground where Jesus had been camped out. "With all his things. Why would he just up and leave?"

Then a thought came to me. An uncomfortable one.

Perhaps I was the reason he left. Maybe he wanted nothing to do with me, so he'd disappeared before I could come back.

But ... surely he couldn't have known I'd come back so soon.

This was a pretty decent spot as far as homeless real estate went. It certainly beat a shop doorway or a park bench. Especially on a beautiful day like this. Why would he give it up?

Then I saw something.

Claw marks cutting through the soil in several places. Deep gouges that I'd seen many times before. In concrete. In the carpet at Granddad's house. Even on the roof of a police car.

Sally's hands rose to her mouth.

She'd seen them, too.

"The robo-dog!" we both said simultaneously. Granddad's robo-dog, K10, had clearly been here and chased Jesus away. Not that it was Granddad's any more. The police had bought it off him. It was theirs now.

But why was it being used to chase homeless people away? And where would Jesus have gone now?

"He can't have gone too far," Sally said, "And we still have these to give him." She dangled the lunch bag in front of me.

"Let's try to find him," I said, leading the way out.

Our bikes still lay in their steely embrace. I spent five minutes trying to remove a pedal from deep inside some spokes, then we set off on a scenic tour of all the town's homeless spots.

It turns out to be more difficult to find a homeless person than you'd think. When you're looking for one, that is. When you're not looking, they seem to be everywhere, like matching socks or sharp pencils.

We tried the bus station, a supermarket car park, even under the flyover, but there wasn't a single homeless person to be found. Not one. Where could they all have gone?

After our second search through town, Sally gestured to a patch of grass surrounding two statues of horses. We laid our bikes on the ground and shared the sandwiches we'd made for Jesus. No point letting them go to waste, and if we returned home with an uneaten picnic, Mum and Dad would launch into a game of Twenty Questions.

"So, where do you think he's gone?" I asked Sally through a mouthful of cheese and ham.

Sally grimaced at a chunk of meat that flew from my mouth and landed in the grass. Then she slowly chewed her food, swallowed and said, "Perhaps the robo-dog is behind it. The police could be using it to clean up the town."

The clatter of metal on stone echoed off the buildings around us and, like a fairy that magically appears when you say its name, the Robo-dog rocketed round the corner and screeched to a halt next to us. Its glowing yellow eyes locked on to Sally and me, its teeth glistening in the afternoon sunlight.

I froze, a half-eaten sandwich suspended inches from my mouth, my heart pounding in my ears. I much preferred it when K10 was on my team.

The metal beast let out a deep growl that sounded like an InSinkErator chewing a teaspoon. Its eyes flashed red.

It was clearly telling us off for something, but what? We weren't doing anything wrong. We were just having a picnic in a public place. Wasn't that allowed?

One of the Taylor twins—our police officer neighbours—jogged around the corner, his shirt hanging out and his moustache drooping. I wasn't surprised he was struggling to keep up with K10's top speed. If it can outrun an ambulance, a police officer on foot didn't stand a chance. Perhaps Granddad should invent some rocket shoes or a jet pack so the police can keep up with it.

The officer came up alongside the robo-dog and leaned forward to catch his breath, his hands resting on his knees.

"Move ... along ... please!" he said, spitting the words out between loud gasps for breath. "This is a ... no-loiter ... zone."

"But it's a public space," Sally said, gesturing to the grass and the benches and the statues. She sounded a lot braver than I felt. "We can have a picnic wherever we want."

"New policy..." the police officer stammered. "Loitering is now restricted to designated places. Like the park.

But that didn't make sense. Because it looked like Jesus had been chased out of the park, too. What was going on?

I stood up and backed away from the robo-dog. I don't mind breaking a few rules here and there, but not when so many teeth are involved.

Sally just sat on the grass, staring up at the police officer. When had she become so defiant? I thought I was the naughty one, and she was the goody-two-shoes. Was this yet another change brought on by her concussion?

The robo-dog was pawing at the ground like a bull about to charge, so I grabbed Sally's arm and helped her to her feet.

"Thanks, Officer Taylor," I said in my politest voice. "We'll be moving along now. Good job keeping the streets so clean."

Then I had a thought. Maybe he could help us find Jesus.

"In fact, you're doing an amazing job. I haven't seen a single homeless person in ages."

The police officer nodded, a proud smile crossing his face. "Yes, well. Our new policy has eradicated homelessness almost entirely."

"But where have they all gone? I mean ... if they're not on the street, then where are they?"

He stared at me, his expression blank.

I held his eye, and he shifted from foot to foot.

"Well, they ... um..." he said, pulling at his moustache, "they're gone. They're no longer clogging up our streets. That's the important thing."

"But that doesn't answer the question," Sally said, stepping up beside me. "Where are they now?"

"What does it matter?" the police officer barked, folding his arms. "As long as they're invisible, everyone's happy."

"Come on, Katy!" he said, looking at the robo-dog and slapping his thigh. "Time to go!"

Katy? Seriously? Wouldn't Killer have been a better name? Or Gnasher?

We grabbed our bikes and stood there watching the police officer walk off with the robo-dog at heel.

"What are they up to?" Sally asked, nodding at their backs.

"I've got no idea," I said, swinging my leg over my bike and sitting down. "But why don't we follow them and find out?

Run Out of Town

I peered around the corner of McDonald's, ignoring the stares from the family eating at the window right next to me.

"Can you see anything?" Sally asked, standing behind me, holding my bike.

"They're just walking along, sniffing in doorways and peering into rubbish bins," I said. "They're definitely looking for something, so maybe Jesus managed to get away."

"Or they could be searching for other homeless people to add to their hoard?"

As the words left her mouth, the robo-dog bolted over to the children's play area and ducked down in its ready-to-pounce mode. The Taylor twin rushed after it, probably worried that it was about to swallow a small child whole. A dirty face appeared in the playhouse's window. An old lady cocooned in filthy blankets rubbed her eyes as though she thought she was still dreaming. Or having a nightmare.

What was with Sally today? Whenever she mentioned something, it happened. Perhaps I should get her to suggest some Lotto numbers?

"They've got one," I said, passing the words back over my shoulder. "A lady sleeping in the little kids' playground."

The robo-dog let out a deep rumbling growl that echoed off the surrounding buildings, and the police officer said something to the lady that I couldn't hear. She slid down the bright blue slide, where the Taylor twin took her by the arm and led her off, K10 trotting along at heel.

"They're heading towards the post office. We should follow them."

I glanced back at Sally, who was already sitting on her bike, holding mine beside her.

"Oh, um, thanks," I said, hopping on my bike and following Sally around the corner. I thought we'd duck from doorway to doorway with our collars up, like they do in the movies. Perhaps wearing dark sunglasses and wide-brimmed hats. But Sally pulled out onto the road in plain sight and headed straight towards our target.

"Hey," I said, trying to get her attention. What was she doing? Shouldn't we stay out of sight and watch where they take her?

Sally did pretty much the opposite. She cycled straight past them, smiling at the policeman and the poor homeless lady, who still looked half asleep. I kept my gaze glued to the road in front of me, trying not to look too guilty.

Then Sally pulled up onto the kerb, leaned her bike against the wall and joined the queue for the cash machine outside the bank.

Smart.

From here we could see exactly what they were doing, without having to hide.

I joined Sally in the queue, raising my eyebrows and nodding slowly.

The cop held tight to the lady's arm, leading her up the street. They stopped next to a police van, and he opened the back door. On command, the dog hopped in. Then the Taylor twin opened the side door and guided the homeless lady inside. A minute later, the police van pulled away. When it got to the end of the street, it didn't turn left towards the police station. It went right, disappearing around the corner.

"Oh, darn," Sally said, patting herself down the way Dad does every time he leaves the house. "I forgot my wallet."

The other people in the queue didn't bat an eyelid as Sally and I mounted our bikes and rode off.

"Where do you think he took her?" I asked Sally as we peddled back home.

"I dunno. Maybe we should follow them to find out!"

"How are we going to do that?" I said, but then an idea came to me. "Ooh, we could..."

Sally nodded, then we spoke at the same time.

"Pretend to be homeless!"

"Use the invisibility collar!"

We both laughed.

The first idea was mine. We could wear grubby clothes, loiter in a doorway, and see where they took us.

Sally squinted, tilting her head to the side. "I think they're both good ideas," she said.

15

Raise a Stink

"Eww, it stinks!" Sally said, holding the dirty orange sleeping bag between thumb and forefinger. She dangled it at arm's length, then slid down the blue slide, going super-fast in Dad's old gardening clothes.

She plopped onto her bum on the rubbery surface of the playground. DaVinci leapt forward, giving her a big slobbery lick on the face. Then he sniffed at the homeless lady's sleeping bag, let out a whine, and hid behind my legs.

I pinched my lips together, trying not to laugh.

"If you laugh, I'll literally kill you!" Sally said, sounding like her old self. She got to her feet, grimacing at her grubby oversized clothes and holding the sleeping bag as far from her nose as she could. "And it won't seem so funny in five minutes when you're butt naked."

She had a point.

My schoolbag hung over my shoulder, containing nothing but the invisibility collar. The plan was to swap it with my clothes, and for Sally to take the bag with her. That way, once we found Jesus and figured out what was going on with all the homeless people, I'd be able to take the collar off and get dressed. On second thoughts, I'd get dressed first, then take the collar off. Being naked while invisible was going to be bad enough.

In fact, I had wanted to be the homeless one, but Sally said I was too young. Social security would be called. Then we'd have some serious explaining to do with Mum and Dad. But then again, perhaps she was saying that because it meant she wouldn't have to take her clothes off?

Instead, Sally put on Dad's old gardening gear and I got to be Mr-Invisible-Nudey-Bum. We hadn't planned on bringing DaVinci along, but we'd told Mum and Dad we were walking into town and they insisted we take him with us. But I'd found a length of rope in the shed instead of a lead, and with the dried mud from the pond still caking his fur, DaVinci actually added to the homeless vibe.

We walked away from the playground, DaVinci tugging on his rope as we looked for a suitable spot to loiter.

It didn't take long.

The dark alleyway beside the Chinese restaurant looked inviting—in a homelessness kind of way. We ducked behind the bins and found a thick bed of cardboard already laid out for us, as though someone had slept here recently. It even smelt the part, especially with the bins and sleeping bag adding to the overall aroma.

Sally dropped the sleeping bag onto the cardboard and put her feet inside, only as far as her ankles. Her nose wrinkled and she looked like she was about to vomit.

"You need to go a bit deeper undercover than that!" I said, nodding at her feet.

She grabbed the sleeping bag between finger and thumb, like she was handling a dead rat, and pulled it up to her knees. "That's as far as I'm willing to go," she said nasally, sounding as though she had a clothes peg on her nose.

"Take this, too," I said, handing her the end of the rope. She tugged DaVinci towards her, but he refused to go anywhere near the sleeping bag. He just sat on the edge of the cardboard, his tongue flopping out of the side of his mouth.

"If any of my friends see me like this, I'll die!"

I glanced over my shoulder as if I'd seen something. "Oh, hi, Steve!" I said theatrically.

"Very funny! Now get on with your side of the deal. I need cheering up."

I grunted and slung my schoolbag from my shoulder, looking around. Bins lined one side of the alleyway, and two old TVs leaned against the opposite wall. A cat loitered at the far end, looking our way, but otherwise the place was deserted. This was as good a spot as any, I guessed.

I pulled the collar out of the bag, turning it around in my hands. Was I really going to do this? In public?

Sally smiled for the first time since she'd put on those skanky clothes. "Come on, Fingers ... you'll be fine!" she said encouragingly. "Do it for Jesus. So we can find out what happened to him. And help him."

Argh, she had a point. Jesus wouldn't have been living on the street if it wasn't for me. Then the police wouldn't have taken him. It was all my fault, yet I wasn't even prepared to step out of my comfort zone. Or my pants.

Letting out a deep sigh, I flicked the switch on the collar. It vibrated in my hand like an electric toothbrush. I put it around my neck and threaded the buckle through, pulling it tight.

Okay, here goes.

I held my hands in front of my face as though I was reading my palms, trying to get a glimpse into my future.

And then it felt like someone turned the lights on in the alleyway. I was looking at a faded Coke can on the ground ... through my hands. My jersey sleeves were hollow, as though filled with nothing but air.

"Woah, that's totally freaky!" Sally said.

"Woof woof," DaVinci added, and he nestled in behind Sally as though terrified of me.

I guess that meant my head had disappeared, too, so I pulled my T-shirt and jersey off together and shoved them in the bag. Then my shoes and socks.

At that point, I hesitated.

"Take it all off, sunshine!" Sally said, her face lit up with glee.

"Very funny, hobo!" I said, undoing the top button of my jeans. Then I stopped again. It felt so wrong. Getting naked. In public. It went against every fibre in my body, even if those fibres were invisible right now.

"Seriously, Finn. Granddad's robo-cop-dog could be here at any moment."

As I undid my fly, the sound of metal pounding concrete came from nearby, getting louder with each beat.

Oh no... Prophet Sally had done it again.

I pulled my trousers and undies down, stepping out of them and shoving them into the bag.

Sally grabbed the bag, zipping it up and clutching it to her chest in a terrified embrace. DaVinci gave a high-pitched whine.

I glanced behind me. No wonder they were scared.

The robo-dog stood in the entrance to the alley, its yellow eyes trained on Sally and DaVinci. Its teeth glistened in the afternoon sunlight and its claws jabbed the ground. Then its nostrils dilated and its head turned so it was looking straight at me. Or through me.

Did it know I was here? Perhaps it had heat or x-ray or thermal vision or something. It's possible. I hadn't got through even half of K10's features when my mind took it for a spin.

It robo-sniffed again.

"Can't we just stay here?" Sally said, as if talking to a human. "I don't want to move on!" The robo-dog sniffed again, then turned its attention back to Sally.

Phew.

I slowly stepped away, pressing my back up against the alley wall, the cold brick against my butt giving me a full-body shiver.

The Taylor twin arrived beside K10, gasping for breath. He looked Sally up and down.

"Ah, good, you've found another one!"

He didn't seem to recognise her from earlier. Although to be fair, I would probably have walked past her without a second glance, and she's my sister. Dad's dirty old clothes hung off her, making her appear skinny and undernourished, and the beanie covered up her new haircut. She'd rubbed a handful of dirt from our flowerbed into her skin, making her look like she hadn't washed in weeks. And she smelled like it, too. No one would suspect that she wasn't homeless.

"Stand up, young lady. And bring your dog," the police officer said. "You're coming with us."

16

Step on It

Sally crossed her arms defiantly. "I don't want to go anywhere. We're fine here."

"It's for your own good," the Taylor twin said, his voice calm but firm. Authoritative, like Mr Miller at school. The robo-dog let out a menacing growl, as though playing good-cop, bad-cop.

Sally clutched the bag with my clothes tighter to her chest and stood up, not taking her eyes off K10.

"Don't forget your things," the cop said, nodding towards the grubby sleeping bag.

"It's fine," Sally said, jiggling the bag in one hand and DaVinci's rope-leash in the other. Then she followed the police officer and robo-dog out of the alleyway, dragging DaVinci behind her.

I took a deep breath, then joined them on the main street. It was really cold, even with the sun still high in the sky. Probably because a breeze was blowing where the sun doesn't shine.

Boy, did I miss my clothes!

The cop walked the same way he'd taken the old homeless lady earlier. The police van was parked up ahead, this time on the other side of the road. Rather than lagging behind, I crossed over and ran on in front. I needed to be there when the doors opened, so I didn't get left behind.

Pebbles bit into the soles of my feet as I ran, and the wind blew, well, everywhere. But in some ways, it was quite freeing. I felt like a wild animal. Or a caveman.

I rushed past an old lady with a walking frame who took up half the pavement. As I ducked onto the grass, it compressed beneath my feet in perfect footprints. It felt nicer than the concrete, but it might give me away if I wasn't careful.

A mother pushed a pram along a bit further ahead, two small children clinging to the side of it. I waited behind them, not wanting to step onto the grass again.

Sally, DaVinci, and the cop weren't far away now.

"Look, Mummy!" one of the kids said, tugging at his mum's dress. "A robot doggy!"

Sure enough, the robot doggy was heading this way, its nostrils dilating like a hunting hound picking up a scent. Please don't let it be hunting me.

The mother picked up her pace, rushing the kids ahead. Everyone in town knew that Granddad's robo-dog was part of the police force, as it had been all over the news. But that didn't make it less scary.

When we arrived at the van, the family hurried on and I stepped off the footpath into a driveway.

How was I going to do this? I couldn't climb into the back with the robo-dog. And if I sat beside Sally, DaVinci would go nuts and might give me away.

K10 reached the van first and sat behind it, facing this way like a lioness guarding her cubs. Its glowing eyes scanned the driveway, its nostrils dilating. Did it know I was here?

The van's orange lights flashed twice, then the Taylor twin opened the back door and the robo-dog hopped in, out of sight.

"Where are you taking us?" Sally asked. "The police station?"

"What? No." The officer said. "We're going to get you cleaned up and fed."

"Oh," Sally said, her eyes lighting up with surprise.

My invisible jaw dropped open.

Seriously?

Of all the things we'd thought they might be doing to Jesus and the other homeless people, that hadn't been one of them. In fact, giving them a bath and a decent meal hadn't even featured in the top ten.

Did we even need to be here? One of us stinking like a rubbish bin, the other as naked as a peeled banana. Perhaps Jesus would be okay.

But he still didn't have a job or a home. And that was all my fault.

True, the police taking him in was definitely better than living on the street, but we still needed to find him and help him get his life back.

The police officer slid the van door open, and Sally had to shove DaVinci inside. Then the officer guided Sally in, making sure she didn't bang her head or make a run for it.

I stepped onto the grass verge, hoping to hop in after Sally, but there was only the slightest gap beside the Taylor twin. Should I try to squeeze through? What if he moved and bumped into me? I peered under his arm and hesitated. DaVinci was curled up on Sally's lap, quivering with fear. The robo-dog sat in the caged area just behind them, its glowing eyes looking this way. Even if I got past the police officer, I'd be only inches from DaVinci's and K10's noses. Surely one of them would give me away? And I'd have nowhere to run.

The door slid shut and the policeman spun around and stepped towards the front of the vehicle. And right on my big toe.

I squeezed my lips together and clamped my hands over my mouth to stop a yelp from

escaping, my butt pressing against the cold metal of the van.

The police officer stopped, looking at the ground to see what he'd stepped on. I lifted all my toes in the air, including the throbbing one. I didn't want to leave perfect footprints in the grass. He paused for a moment, pulling at his moustache. How could he not hear my heart pounding? It was louder than a helicopter.

He gave one last confused glance at the ground, then opened the driver's door and hopped in.

I was still rubbing my sore toe when the engine started up.

No!

I was about to be left behind. Sally, DaVinci, and my clothes were getting taken who-knew-where. Leaving me standing on the pavement, completely naked.

17. Hang On

The police van shuddered, its engine revving.

What should I do?

I stared at Sally, willing her to do something, even though she couldn't see me and probably didn't know where I was. But it seemed to work. Sally pulled at the doorhandle on the inside.

Nothing happened.

I guess that made sense. The police didn't want criminals being able to hop out, willy-nilly. But I couldn't open the door from the outside, or the policeman would freak out.

Sally's lips moved as she spoke to the officer. What was she saying? I think she was trying to buy me time.

Time to do what?

I clearly couldn't get in the vehicle with her.

What about on it?

I stared up at the van's roof. It was high. Really high. There was a steel bar spanning the width of it, with blue and red lights on top. At least I'd have something to hold on to.

But it was so high. And I was completely naked except for Granddad's stupid collar. I didn't want to think what would happen if I fell from up there. That time I came off my skateboard in shorts and a T-shirt had been bad enough.

Yet my sister and DaVinci were inside. I couldn't let them be taken away, even if they were just getting cleaned up.

No. I had to do this.

The back and sides were too steep, so I rushed to the front and looked up at the sloping metal and the windscreen. It started moving towards me.

Argh! I was about to be run over by a police van!

Hopping backwards on one foot, I placed the other on the grille next to the number plate. Then I reached up and grabbed a windscreen wiper, just as the van pulled out onto the road.

An icy breeze blew on my butt, practically chilling me from the inside out, but I didn't have time to be cold. Shops and houses sped past as I shot down the street backwards, clinging on to my life with my fingers and toes.

I couldn't hang on for long. Already the pain was unbearable.

Carefully raising my left foot onto the bonnet, I placed it on the 'P' of police, and stood up on the front of the vehicle.

Just as it turned a corner.

I yelped and fell forward, my hands and face splatting into the windscreen like the world's largest fly.

I panted, trying to catch my breath. The glass misted up beside my mouth and a clammy hand print appeared beneath my invisible fingers.

Oops.

Behind it, I could see the police officer staring right through me as he drove along. He didn't seem to have noticed. Sally, on the other hand, stared wide-eyed at my face, her forehead knitted like a woolly jumper. Her lips moved as she said something to the police officer, while waving her arms around. She was clearly trying to distract him.

I didn't have long.

Pushing off the windscreen, I lunged up and grabbed hold of the police lights with both arms. The rest of my naked body lay flat against the windscreen, its coldness pricking my skin like needles.

Fortunately, the collar still hummed away at my throat. Which meant they couldn't see me. But if my hands were forming misty palmprints, I dreaded to think what shapes Sally and the police officer could see right now!

It must have been something unpleasant, because there was a firm thwack on my left thigh, like I'd been hit with a ruler.

Then the right thigh.

Then left again.

Oh no! The police officer had turned the windscreen wipers on, trying to fling me off like a dead bug.

Ow!

That really hurt.

No way was I hanging around getting my bum wiped. I took off, scrambling up the windscreen and onto the roof of the vehicle. Glancing behind me to check there were no low bridges coming up, I stepped over the police lights.

For a brief second, I stood there surfing the police van as it hurtled down the street, its lights flashing between my invisible legs. Then Mum's voice echoed inside my head, using words like 'reckless' and 'stupid', so I dropped down on my front, gripping the steel bar. The problem was the lights flashed right in my face, so brightly it stung. Squinting was useless with invisible eyelids, so I pressed my face into the hard white roof. That's how I spent the rest of the journey: lying on cold metal with wind rushing over my naked skin, wondering how the heck I always got myself into these crazy situations.

18

Home In

When the van slowed to a stop, I could have cried with relief.

Cold.

So, so cold.

My whole body shuddered along with the invisibility collar. My teeth chattered and my muscles ached from being clenched for so long.

But I'd made it.

We were there. Wherever there was.

I looked up from the white roof and glanced around. We were on the edge of town, in a place

I didn't recognise. Large houses lined the street, with glimpses of rolling green countryside between each building.

The front door of the van clunked shut, sending yet more vibrations through my body. Then the back door slid open.

Sally rushed out, dragging DaVinci along behind her. As soon as the police officer looked the other way, she peered up at the roof, her eyes wide with worry.

I nodded and waved, before remembering I was invisible. Instead, I gave one sharp tap on the roof with my finger. The police officer turned towards me, looking confused, but Sally visibly relaxed, scratching DaVinci behind his ear, then swinging the bag of clothes onto her shoulder.

Oh, how I wished I was wearing those clothes right now.

But I didn't have time to lie there, fantasising about getting warm. The Taylor twin was leading Sally and DaVinci towards a large house with three chimneys rising from its steep, shingled roof.

I clambered down the windscreen, finding this direction much easier. Especially since it was stationary, the wipers weren't whacking me, and a police officer wasn't staring out through the glass. K10's eyes still glowed in the back of the van, but I didn't care, as long as it was locked away.

I hopped down, wincing as gravel poked at my cold feet, then rushed after Sally, who was being led into the building. I ducked inside, just as the heavy wooden door clunked shut behind me. Rough wallpaper scratched my back, but I was glad to be in the dim light of inside for a change.

The odour of cleaning products and air-freshener hit me, but it was masking undertones of something that smelled like the homeless sleeping bag.

DaVinci jumped up at Sally, rushing around her and tying her in the rope. I think he was just pleased to be away from the robo-dog. It's always freaked him out, ever since Granddad first invented it.

The Taylor twin led them along the dim hallway, through large double doors. I followed a few metres behind, wooden floorboards creaking beneath my feet.

What was this place? It looked like it had once been a fancy home or even a hotel, but was now a bit run down. Antique furniture filled every nook, and creepy old paintings lined the walls.

We turned into a bright room and I stopped in the doorway, blinded. When my eyes adjusted, I stared at the scene in amazement. There must have been ten people in the room, mostly sitting in armchairs, staring at a large TV on the far wall. They were all a bit scruffy. Eccentric is what Mum would have called them. The lady closest to me was shoving an enormous cream donut into her mouth, as though trying to eat it before anyone could take it from her. She looked familiar. Her recently washed hair stuck to the side of her head, and she wore a pristine white dressing gown.

Then it hit me.

She was the homeless lady from the playground. The one whose sleeping bag Sally had borrowed. We'd thought she was getting carted off to her doom, but here she was, in a warm, donut-eating paradise.

What about Jesus? Was he here, too?

I scanned the room, taking in dreadlocks and tattoos and tired eyes.

Then I saw him.

Jesus. Hey-ZEUS.

He sat in an armchair in front of a fire, a teacup clenched in his hands as though it was his most treasured possession.

Phew. He was okay. In fact, he was better than okay. A huge smile filled his face, rather than the usual grumpy frown.

A no-nonsense nurse rushed over to Sally, who was also staring wide-eyed at Jesus. The lady nodded at the police officer, saying, "Thanks, Tom." Then she turned to Sally. "I'm Nurse Hardy, the charge nurse. Let's get you a quick cup of tea and a bite to eat, then I have some forms for you to fill in. After that, we'll get you and your dog cleaned up."

What had we even been worried about? This place was a homeless person's paradise. In fact, it was also an invisible-naked-person's paradise! There were several empty armchairs near the fire, so I crept over and lowered myself onto the furthest chair from Jesus.

I sat there basking in the warmth, with a great view of the room.

The nurse scratched DaVinci behind the ear, then ushered Sally to a table by the window and gave her a plateful of sandwiches. Sally picked one up and ate it normally, without the frenzy of someone who hadn't eaten a decent meal in weeks. If she wanted to blend in, she needed to get into character.

I looked back at Jesus, a few chairs away. His feet only just reached the floor and the back of the tall chair rose over his head, like he was a small child. He rocked back and forward, clearly very content. His hair had been washed and brushed, his beard trimmed to almost nothing. He looked like the security guard I remembered, except happier. He probably didn't even want his old job back.

So, this was what had happened to all the town's homeless people? They'd been taken away to be fed and cleaned up. We'd been worried about them, but they were fine.

Perhaps I should go and get Sally. Make a run for it. Once outside, I could put my clothes back on and we could catch a bus home. Easy.

Jesus waved his hand, looking over his shoulder. "Yo, Doc! Hook a brotha up with some more of them sammies, will ya? I ain't had grub that good in a hot minute."

My mouth dropped open.

What had happened to Hey-ZEUS's accent? It had completely gone. Replaced by what? Street talk. But he'd only been on the street for a few weeks. In fact, just that morning he'd sounded like his normal self.

The nurse strode over and handed him a plate piled high with sandwiches. "Here you go, Reggie."

Jesus took the plate and smiled, shaking his head from side to side. "That's mighty fine, sunshine! You brightenin' up my day, no lie."

Reggie?

Sunshine?

What the heck was happening here?

19.
On Present form

"Psst! Sally!" I hissed, right into her ear.

She snorted, spraying tea out of her nostrils. Then she spluttered and coughed, with more tea cascading down Dad's gardening shirt.

Oops.

I stepped to the side as Nurse Hardy rushed over and wiped both Sally and the table down.

"Let me take that," the nurse said, picking up a tea-splattered form. Her eyes scanned over it. "Angela Swindon, yes? And you're eighteen years old? No immediate family. Perfect. And what's your dog's name?"

Sally and I looked at DaVinci, whose front paws were resting on the arm of a chair while a bearded old man fed him a donut.

"Da..." Sally stuttered. "Um... Dav... Dave."

"Oh, my husband's called Dave," the nurse said, and Sally's face flushed pink. "What a lovely name for a dog. Well, finish up those sandwiches, Angela, and we'll get you cleaned up downstairs."

Sally smiled and the nurse left, so I tried again.

"Sorry!" I whispered, not directly into her ear this time. "It's only me."

"I know it's you," she said in a hushed voice. "I didn't think I had any other invisible brothers here! I just didn't know you were only a millimetre away from my ear!"

"Sorry," I said again, "but something strange is going on. I've found Jesus. But it's not him. I mean ... it looks like him. It's his body. But..."

I didn't know what else to say. What could have changed him in such a short time? Unless...

"You think he's swapped bodies?" Sally asked.

I nodded, staring at her blank face.

Then I remembered I was invisible and added, "Yes."

Sally placed her hand in front of her mouth and spoke again, her voice barely audible. "But why would they be doing that? This all seems so normal. And nice."

"And warm!" I added. I couldn't forget the warmth.

"Oh, can you help me with these?" Sally asked, nodding towards the sandwiches. "I'm supposed to be a starving street kid, but we've already had two lunches."

I glanced around the room. I'm sure DaVinci would have been her first choice, but he was dashing from seat to seat, getting spoilt rotten by homeless people who suddenly had surplus food.

Anyway, I was a bit peckish, and no one was facing this way, except a man with dark, weather-beaten skin a few chairs over. But his eyes stared into the distance, as though watching TV in another dimension.

Ducking around to the other side of the table, I grabbed an egg sandwich. I kept it low to the plate so no one could see it hovering and took a big mouthful. After chewing for a few seconds, I swallowed and looked down. Mushy bits of egg hung in mid-air, making their way towards my invisible stomach. As I stared at them, they disappeared into nothingness.

"That is the grossest thing I have ever seen!" Sally said, as I took another massive bite.

I glanced at the staring man, but he couldn't have noticed or else he'd have run away screaming. As it was, his expression hadn't changed at all, so I carefully finished the whole plate of sandwiches.

Just as I shoved the last half in my mouth, the man tilted his head to the side, his gaze resting on me. Or at least, on where I should have been. I quickly swallowed, the huge lump of barely chewed food bulging my throat on its way down and reminding me of DaVinci. I held my hands in front of my chest in a futile attempt to hide the floating mushy paste that was suspended there.

Without speaking, the man pushed himself up from his chair and headed this way. He had a scar above one eyebrow and his wiry black hair was sprinkled with flecks of white, even though he didn't look that old.

I held my breath, partly from fear of what he might do and partly due to the stabbing pain of indigestion in my chest. I really should have chewed my food.

The man sat on the chair next to Sally and the corners of his mouth rose into a half-smile, half-frown.

He leaned forward, put his hand over his lips and spoke so quietly I could only just make out the words. "You ze girl from ze hospital, no? With ze granddad? And your inveeseeeble brother ees here too, no?"

Sally's jaw dropped open. "Jesus?"

"You say eet Hey-ZEUS!"

Oh my days! I was right. They had swapped bodies. That was certainly Jesus's mind in this other man's body. But why? What was this place?

"What's happened to you, Hey-ZEUS?' Sally whispered. "You're ... um ... not looking like yourself."

"They said they ees needing to test. They give food and shelter, if we test for them. But I should know you two do thees, with your crazy eenvensions."

"What? No!" I said. "We came here to find you."

Sally shot me an I-can-handle-this glare and said, "We want to help you get your job back, Hey-ZEUS. We're here to help."

Jesus stared at Sally for a moment, his usual frown looking foreign on this stranger's face.

He nodded. "Well, zen, get me out of here. But first, I need my body back."

The nurse strolled over and picked up the empty plate from in front of Sally.

"Well done, Angela," she said. Then she smiled at Jesus. "And I see you've met the lovely Hey-ZEUS! Maybe he can look after Dave while we get you cleaned up?"

We all looked over at DaVinci, who had a nurse pinned against the wall and was eating cookies straight off her tray.

I stifled a laugh as Jesus rushed over to help, then tiptoed along behind Sally as she was led from the room. If these guys were swapping people's minds, I didn't want to let Sally out of my sight.

20
Sounds Like a Plan

Nurse Hardy led us down some stairs into a long basement corridor with doors lining either side. It smelled dank and musty, like DaVinci's bedding after he'd been swimming in the duck pond.

She opened one of the doors, revealing a brightly lit, white-tiled room with shower curtains hanging in the corner.

A towel and bathrobe sat on a table beside the door, both fluffy and white like marshmallows.

"Here you are, Angela. Get yourself cleaned up. Take as long as you like."

Sally picked up the towel and closed the door behind herself, leaving me alone in the corridor with the nurse, who gave a wide smile and rubbed her hands together like a Bond villain.

Then she strode along the corridor and opened another door. Light spilled out over the faded carpet.

She spoke into the room in a loud whisper. "I've got her. She's in the shower now."

"Will anyone miss her?" replied a croaky old lady's voice. It sounded oddly familiar.

"No, ma'am," the nurse said, shuffling further into the room. "She's perfect. Homeless and alone, but still very young, and I'd say quite pretty, once we've cleaned her up. I daresay you couldn't ask for better."

My heart thumped in my chest as I tiptoed closer to the doorway.

What did they want with Sally? Perfect for what?

A groan of pain came from the room, and perhaps the creak of a bed. "Well, hurry. I don't know how long I have left."

"Everything's ready to go," Nurse Hardy said, peering right through me at the room where Sally was showering. "We can do it the moment she comes out of the shower. Should I talk to her first, like we did with the others?"

"No!" the voice said firmly. "This one won't be so keen once she realises what's in it for her. Let's keep her down here, away from the others."

"She seemed to be getting friendly with another guest. Hey-ZEUS, the Colombian."

"Okay, good to know. I'll stay out of his way once I've made the switch."

"What should I do with the rest of the guests?"

"I'm finished with them. After I'm done with the machine, get my body out of here. Then get them back into their own wretched bodies and let them go."

"Back to the streets, ma'am?"

"Whatever. I'll have what I need."

The sound of rushing water came from the bathroom. Sally was still in the shower, blissfully unaware of what was being plotted out here.

But what was being plotted?

Even I wasn't sure and I'd heard the whole conversation. An old lady wanted something from Sally. But what? And there was some kind of machine involved.

Whatever they planned, they were going to do it as soon as Sally finished her shower.

After a few moments' silence, the nurse spoke again. "We could…" She hesitated. "Um … keep the facility open. Now that the initial investment has been made."

"Oh, I don't care about homeless people any more. Politics is long behind me. I just wanted to make sure the machine worked and find myself a new body. One that wouldn't be missed. And now that I have one, I couldn't give a guinea pig's bottom what happens to the rest of them."

Nurse Hardy's jaw hung open for a few seconds, before she snapped it shut. "Very well, ma'am," she said, then turned and walked away.

Directly towards me!

I leapt back, pressing my butt cheeks against the wall, and she missed me by millimetres.

Phew, that was close.

The nurse stopped outside the shower room, got her phone out of her pocket, and tapped away at the screen.

Knowing Sally's bathroom habits, she might be waiting a while. Days, even.

I glanced back up the corridor at the other room. The nurse had left the door ajar. Maybe I could figure out exactly what was going on before Sally finished up?

Before peering into the room, my hand crept up to my collar, feeling the buzzing on my fingertips. Checking its pulse for signs of life, so I don't suddenly become visibly naked.

I squeezed myself through the gap in the door. The handle bumped my chest and the door creaked, but it could have been the wind.

My eyes took a few seconds to adjust to the gloom.

A hospital wheely-bed sat in the far corner, its large headboard fitted with dials and monitors and other equipment.

At first glance, it appeared empty. Then I spotted a shock of curly white hair above pale wrinkly skin. A pair of hollow, sunken eyes looked straight through me.

Mrs Taylor!

Our neighbour and mother to the twin police officers.

That's whose voice I'd heard.

The kind old lady who used to give us baking and a Christmas card. Who was once mayor of the town and an important figure in Cambridge.

She's the one plotting to use Sally for something?

"Hullo?" she croaked. "Nurse Hardy?"

I froze, my heart thumping in my ears.

Then I saw a strange invention on the wall beside Mrs Taylor's bed and let out a faint gasp.

Two robo-dog heads pointed away from each other, like a trophy from a mutant-robo-hunt. Their mouths hung open as if in mid-roar, and a computer keyboard was mounted below them on a wooden plaque.

I stared at the weird display, my mind spinning.

Had Granddad made that?

It certainly looked like one of his inventions. No, wait. It looked like two of Granddad's inventions. A blend of his mind-swapping machine and his robo-dog. The robo-dog heads had been used instead of the record-player funnels of his previous mind-swapper.

Surely Granddad wasn't behind this?

No.

He couldn't be. He was at home cleaning himself up after his dip in the pond.

And this collar was the only thing he'd been working on since he'd sold the robo-dog designs to the police.

So, had Mrs Taylor stolen his plans and merged his two inventions together?

That's what it looked like.

The old lady groaned and her eyes drooped shut, as if she might cark it at any second. Although with the sharp metallic teeth inches from her skull, she looked like she might become robo-dog food the moment she did.

The other metal head pointed towards a wooden chair with a high back and arm straps.

Oh.

I suddenly got it.

That's what Mrs Taylor was up to. She wanted to steal my sister's body.

And let Sally die in her old body.

No way was that happening.

Not on my watch!

 21. In Full Swing

The door swung open and Nurse Hardy led Sally into the room. Her clean skin glimmered under the strip lighting and she wore fresh clothes. The white blouse still had fold-lines, as if straight from the packet. And it looked more like Mum's style than Sally's. Although, with her new haircut, she looked stylish—and not at all like Mum.

Sally's eyes took in the room, flitting from the robo-dog-mind-swapper to the chair directly below it, then to the bed. Her eyes widened when she saw Mrs Taylor lying there, recognition lighting up her features.

Her lips moved as if about to say something like, "It's you!" or "Mrs Taylor!"

But fortunately, no words came out. She just stared at the old lady.

Behind her, the nurse fiddled with a small brown bottle, holding it upside down over a cloth. Then she screwed the lid back on the bottle and slipped it in her pocket. Sally turned to face her, and Nurse Hardy gave a half smile, before pressing her cloth-filled hand over Sally's nose and mouth. Sally's eyes widened for a second, before drooping shut as her body slumped.

I watched in horror as the nurse caught Sally and carried her towards the wooden chair.

She was going to be mind-swapped with Mrs Taylor.

Right now.

If I didn't do something, Sally would be stuck in Mrs Taylor's body. Which would be like trading

a new sports car for a rusty old go-kart. One that might fall apart at any moment.

I couldn't let that happen.

As the nurse plunked Sally down in the wooden chair, I rushed across the room, the cool basement air chilling my naked skin.

My first obstacle was the nurse's butt. She hunched over Sally, lowering her onto the chair, blocking my route to the robo-dog mind-swapping machine.

Because surely the machine was my only hope. If I damaged it somehow, they wouldn't be able to swap bodies.

I held my breath, squeezed past the nurse, and reached up to the closest robo-dog-head. Standing on tiptoes, I could just reach its lower jaw, so I threaded my fingers between its teeth.

When the nurse turned away, I yanked on the head to see if I could pull it off or point it away from Sally.

It didn't budge.

It was like trying to pull a branch from a tree trunk.

I lifted my legs so my entire weight was hanging from the robo-jaw, just as the nurse tied a strap around Sally's waist and tightened it. Once Sally was secure, the nurse stepped back, glancing between Sally, slumped forward in her chair, and Mrs Taylor, lying in the hospital bed. She clasped her hands together and stepped towards the keyboard.

Oh no!

My head was only inches from the robo-mouth. If it activated now, I'd probably end up in Mrs Taylor's body. And Mrs Taylor would be a naked, invisible eleven-year-old boy. Which was more than she'd bargained for.

I swung my legs from side to side, gaining momentum with each swing. The robo-head wobbled, but didn't give way.

Come on! Come on!

Even if the jaw fell off, it would be something. It might stop the nurse from typing on the keyboard. Although, if she reached out to type at the wrong moment, my butt would stop her. Who would get the biggest shock? Her or me?

I tucked my knees up by my ears and swung harder, like an invisible pendulum.

Above Sally.

Above Mrs Taylor.

Sally..

Mrs Taylor.

Pain flared in my fingers as they dug into the rough edges of the robo-mouth.

The nurse took a deep breath, then slowly raised her right hand.

My fingers slipped from the robo-head.

In slow motion, the nurse stretched out her index finger and jabbed it towards the keyboard.

Just as I fell in front of her.

Ow!

She poked me right in the eye.

But if I hadn't let go, she'd have jabbed me somewhere even less comfortable!

As it was, my butt slammed into the cold, hard floor, knocking the wind out of me. I rolled onto my side, gasping for breath, both invisible hands clamped over my sore eye.

Even with my hands over my face, I could still see the nurse looking around the room.

She carefully examined her index finger, which glistened with one of my teardrops. She held it to her nose and sniffed, her blank face showing me that it didn't smell. Which would have been a different story if my fingers hadn't slipped.

I stayed in foetal position on the floor, pressing my eye and looking up as the nurse jabbed her finger forward again. This time, it connected with the keyboard.

P

R

O

I watched helplessly from below as she typed, 'Proceed with direct swap.'

Wow, whoever made this machine had done a better job than Granddad. On the original mind-swapper, we'd had to type, 'Do you need the toilet?'

As soon as she hit the Enter key, a deep growl came from both robo-throats, like wary dogs meeting in the park.

The nurse retreated to the far side of the room. Which was a very good idea. I scrambled on all fours into the closest corner, the sound echoing off the walls. I looked back as the robo-mouths let out a final ferocious roar.

Sally's eyes shot open.

"It worked! Thank goodness," she said, her voice sounding posher than usual. "The pain is gone!"

I studied the old woman lying in the bed for signs of Sally, but the only movement was the steady rise and fall of her breath.

They'd done it.

Mrs Taylor was in Sally's young body. And Sally was a decrepit old lady who didn't have long to live.

22

Make the Call

I cowered in the corner as Sally's body undid the straps and stood up.

She stretched her hands towards the sky, then leaned forward and down, tapping her feet with her fingertips.

"This is wonderful," she said with a smile. "I haven't been able to touch my toes for sixty years!"

The nurse stepped out of the shadows, also smiling. But her smile looked forced, like she'd rather be somewhere else. Or perhaps she didn't fully agree with Mrs Taylor's actions?

"Take my body next door," Sally-Taylor said, flicking her hand in a shooing motion, like there was a fly on her cupcake. "And stop all medication. She won't last more than an hour or two, which is perfect. We need that horrid homeless girl out of the picture."

"Yes, ma'am."

"Then put all of our test subjects back into their own bodies, give them a hundred dollars and drop them outside a liquor store. I want them drunk enough to forget everything that's happened. That way, if they do tell anyone, well ... no one believes a drunk."

"As you wish, ma'am."

Sally-Taylor paused in the doorway. "Oh, one last thing. Once they're all swapped back, destroy that machine. I don't want it ever getting out that this is possible."

She gestured at her body. No ... not her body. My sister's body! Then she marched out of the room.

I stayed in the corner, trying to process what I'd just heard. Mrs Taylor had planned this all along. She used the homeless people to test her mind-swapping machine, because she knew no one would believe them if they talked. And now she'd got what she wanted, she was going to destroy the machine.

A dark thought hit me. Was this all my fault, too? After all, my actions had got Mrs Taylor hospitalised. And when I was inside the robo-dog, I'd leapt over her body in the hospital, seconds before I was swapped back. Did she see that happen? Was that where she'd got the idea from?

I glanced at the door that Sally-Taylor had left through. Then at the nurse, who was standing beside the hospital bed that contained the sleeping old lady and my sister's mind. What was I supposed to do?

My gut told me not to let Sally out of my sight. But which Sally? Mind or body?

The old lady's chest rose and fell. The monitor on the headboard showed her heartbeat, slow but steady. Was Sally still unconscious from having the cloth over her face, or was it from the illness that was killing Mrs Taylor? Who knew?

What I did know was that her mind wasn't going anywhere for now... at least, nowhere I could bring her back from. And if I was going to save my sister, I would need her body.

I took a last glance at old Mrs Taylor, her white hair barely visible against the pillow. The former mayor who was about to die, killing my sister in the process.

No. I had to stop her.

As the nurse began wheeling the hospital bed towards the door, I rushed ahead and stepped into the corridor, just as my sister's body disappeared around the far corner. I broke into a run, landing my feet on the hard floor as softly as I could. Turning the corner, I saw a door closing up ahead, the bright light of the room slowly getting eclipsed. I gave a burst of speed, but wasn't going to make it. It was too far away.

I leapt forward, crashing onto the rough carpet with my naked body, sliding along with my arm outstretched. Just before the light disappeared completely, I hooked my fingers around the door frame, grimacing at the pain, but stopping the door from clicking shut.

I lay there on the floor, quietly panting. Jaw clenched tight against the stinging pain in my knees, hips, elbows, and fingertips.

Ow. Ow. Ow.

Nude diving onto a hard floor was pretty stupid. But I'd done it. I'd stopped the door from closing.

Giving it a gentle push with my thumb, I opened it an inch, before pulling myself along the floor so my ear was right next to the gap. I also tucked my body up against the wall. If anyone walked down the corridor, I didn't want them tripping over me.

For a while, the room was silent, then I heard the click of an old-fashioned phone. One that sits on the desk and doesn't have apps or anything.

"Tim, it's your mother. Codeword? Oh, yes. Rejuvenate."

There was a pause.

"Yes ... it obviously worked. A nice-looking young girl. Eighteen years old. Perfect, really, once I lose this ridiculous nose piercing and get a more sensible haircut. No. Of course she didn't have any documents, just a bag full of boys' clothes. She was homeless. What did you expect? A driver's license? Keys to a Porsche? I have a name and date of birth. Angela Swindon. Twenty-fourth of July, 2007. That will have to do."

Another pause.

"Okay, you do that. And tell your brother to come see me. I have a job for him."

The phone clicked again.

I lay on the floor, resting my head on my arm and breathing softly.

What was I going to do?

The nurse would destroy the mind-swapping machine as soon as she got the homeless people back in their own bodies. And Sally would be trapped as an old lady. For the few hours she had left to live.

How was this possible?

I had been trying to do the right thing. To help Jesus and fix all the other problems that I'd caused.

But I'd gone and made things worse.

Much, much worse.

23

TOP DOG

I'm not sure how long I lay there on the hard floor, shivering, a small damp patch appearing beneath my invisible eyes.

Sounds of life came through the crack in the door. The slow click of computer keys. A pen scratching at paper. A drink being poured.

Whatever Sally-Taylor was doing in there, she wasn't in a hurry. Was she waiting for something? Someone?

As if in answer to my question, a doorhandle clicked at the other end of the corridor. I twisted around to see a uniformed policeman opening the door. It was one of the Taylor twins. Mrs Taylor's son. This must be who she'd asked for on the phone. She had a job for him.

The policeman stood there, holding the door, looking over his shoulder.

Then glowing yellow eyes came into view. I heard the clunk of metal hitting the hard floor.

K10, Granddad's terrifying robo-dog, stepped into the corridor. Its head turned left and right, its nostrils dilating as it picked up a scent.

I scrambled to my feet, pressing my back against the wall, glancing around for something that might save me.

Where should I go?

There were three closed doors on this short stretch of corridor, other than the one next to me with Sally-Taylor behind it. Were they locked? And where did they even go? I didn't want to trap myself in a broom cupboard.

A thick yellow ribbon of light lined the door beside me, but Sally-Taylor was on the other side. If I pushed it open, she might get suspicious.

I slid along the wall, away from the robo-dog, whose head scanned left and right, sniffing the air, its yellow eyes searching for the source of the scent.

"Easy, Katy," the Taylor twin said, his voice firm, commanding. "What's got you spooked?"

My heart thumped against my ribcage, trying to beat its way out of there.

I kept my eyes on the robo-dog's teeth, my back and butt cheeks pressed against the wall as I edged further away.

It lowered its head and sniffed the floor.

Once.

Twice.

Its eyes brightened, clearly sensing something. And that something was me.

Ow!

My shoulder bumped into a sharp corner. A red fire alarm button box with a glass window. The impact only made the slightest sound, but it was enough.

The robo-dog leapt forward, charging straight at me.

I pushed off the wall and sprinted down the corridor with big strides. The sound of my feet pounding the floor was hopefully drowned out by the metal claws of my pursuer.

But where could I go? I was running into a dead end.

I reached the door at the end of the corridor and frantically twisted the handle, but it didn't budge. Spinning around, I pressed myself up against the cold door, as if trying to morph through it.

K10 screeched to a halt a metre from me, its nose sniffing the air between us.

"Get back here, you useless metal mutt," the policeman grumbled, striding towards us. "You know what Sarge said. One more malfunction and you're decommissioned."

The robo-dog edged forward, its nose moving from side to side. Its teeth opening and closing. It was going to reach me at any moment. Those teeth. My bare flesh.

I had to do something.

I glanced at the doorknob beside me. It wouldn't turn, but perhaps it could still save me? Stretching my leg up as far as it would go, I placed my bare foot on the handle. Then I pushed off the inside of the frame, lifting myself up as the dog came closer. A metal arm protruded from the door above my head, probably to stop it from slamming. Stretching as high as I could, I grabbed hold of it with my right hand, and pulled myself up.

My heart rattled my ribcage as I balanced in a naked yoga pose with one foot on the doorknob and my fingers gripping the metal arm above the door.

The robo-dog edged forward, sniffing. If it looked up, it would catch the delightful scent of my naked bum.

The muscles in my arms and legs burned as I held the pose. I couldn't keep this up for much longer.

"What's got into you?" the police officer grumbled, tapping the robo-dog's butt with his toe. "If you don't stand down, I'll report you."

The door halfway down the corridor opened and Sally-Taylor poked her head out, her lips pursed and eyebrows raised.

"Oh, hello, dear," she said to the policeman. "What's going on?"

If Officer Taylor was surprised to hear my sister calling him 'Dear', he didn't show it.

"This blasted thing is malfunctioning again. Honestly. I don't know why we bother."

Cramp flared in my left thigh and right forearm. I gritted my teeth against the pain, as my fingers slipped from the metal bar. Millimetre by millimetre.

Sally-Taylor said something I didn't catch and her son turned to face her, just as my fingers slipped off the bar.

I fell forward, my teeth clamped together to stop me yelping. The robo-butt rushed towards me as I landed on top of K10. My chin thumped into metal, white dots flickering across my vision.

Its tail pressed into my cheek, my legs on either side of its head.

The dog twisted and turned beneath me, trying to pick up my scent, but my legs moved with it, keeping them out of reach of both nose and teeth.

The police officer spun around and looked down at me. Or through me. "This is your last chance!" he said sternly, his black boot rising from the floor and jabbing right towards my nose. I pulled my

head back at the last second and the boot clobbered the ro-butt, as intended. "Heel, now, or I'll dismantle you myself."

The robo-dog turned around, facing towards Sally-Taylor, bringing my face within centimetres of the doorknob which had just saved my life. I could've kissed it. Literally.

Then the door fell out of reach as the robo-dog clunked reluctantly down the corridor with me on its back. Did it even know I was there?

Who cared? I was safe for the time being, my fingers linked under its belly, its cold surface already warming beneath my skin.

I squinted as the robo-dog entered the bright office, but my invisible eyelids did nothing to dim the light.

"Over there. Sit!" the policeman barked and the robo-dog clunked into the middle of the room, turned and sat. My butt rose into the air and my nose pressed into a rug as I koala'd on for dear life, not wanting to slip off from the relative safety of behind-the-teeth. I could sense the robo-dog sniffing the surrounding air, but, at least for now, it was following orders.

"So, what do you think?" Sally-Taylor said from behind her desk, out of view. Sally's voice sounded different. Posher.

The police officer tilted his head to the side. "I don't know. She seems ... um ... familiar."

"Of course she's familiar. You brought her in as a dirty street urchin. But now she's cleaned up, she's perfect. I mean, I'm perfect. I have another seventy years left in me. It's wonderful."

Blood pulsed in my head and a tentacle of dribble stretched out over my cheek. How long could I stay in this upside-down position without passing out? The invisibility collar hummed against my neck, now a calming presence, reminding me I couldn't be seen. But if I passed out on the floor, it could be hours before someone found me. The only people who knew I was invisible were old-Sally, who could cark it at any minute, and Jesus, who was about to be cast back out on the street.

The trill of an old-fashioned phone jerked me out of my thoughts, nearly toppling me from the robo-dog's back. I gripped it tighter, my head twisted at right angles to the rest of my body.

I could hear half of the phone conversation through the ear that wasn't pressed into carpet.

"Hello?"

"Oh, good. Are they the last ones?"

"Wonderful. Destroy the machine as soon as they're done. And how's, erm ... poor old Mrs Taylor?"

"That's ... inconvenient. The doctor's already on his way to declare her dead, so hurry things along, if you have to."

"Okay. Goodbye."

Oh no. That was the nurse she was talking to. And if I understood correctly, she was about to destroy the mind-swapping machine, then kill old-Sally. I couldn't just lie there with my invisible butt in the air. I had to do something!

24

Get a GRIP

I had to get back to the mind-swapping machine.

Right now.

The problem was, I couldn't just stand up and walk out of the room. The door was closed, with Sally-Taylor and her police officer son only a few feet away.

"Can you look at this for me? I've revised the will, making the lucky Angela Swindon my sole beneficiary."

The police officer walked around the other side of the desk and stared at a document.

But I still couldn't make a run for it. The second I hopped off the robo-dog's back, it would sense me and go bonkers again.

So, how the heck could I get out of here?

Unless I made it go bonkers on purpose.

If the police officer thinks it's malfunctioning, he might shut it down.

Okay, so there's also the possibility that he won't and that the robo-dog will sink its teeth into my bare bum. But I didn't have anything else up my sleeve. Or any sleeves, for that matter. All I had was my bare bum and my wits.

"That looks like it's all in order," the Taylor twin said. "Provided she's given you her real name."

"Mmm, I hadn't thought of that. But it wouldn't matter. I'd just need some fake documents that matched the name and I'd be able to claim it."

My jaw dropped open. If I didn't stop her and get Sally back into her own body, she might get away with this. She'd steal my sister's life and still have all her own money and possessions.

No way.

I had to fix this mess. All of these messes.

Pressing both palms into the carpet, I pushed myself up, my lower half still resting on cold metal.

If this were a yoga pose, it would be called Downward Facing Robo-Dog. I twisted my body around, bringing my left leg over the dog's head, so I was facing forward.

The dog's robo-nostrils dilated, its eyes glowing brighter. It sensed something, but for now was still following orders. It just needed a bit more encouragement.

I glanced round the room.

Sally-Taylor picked up the pile of paper from the desk and slipped it into a folder. The police officer stared out of the window.

I needed something to distract the dog.

Something that only it would see.

But there was nothing within reach.

I leaned down and plucked at the carpet, trying to pull off some fluff to dangle in front of the dog. But I couldn't get a strong enough grip. My fingers kept slipping.

"Right, then," Sally-Taylor said, "the will is in order. Once the doctor signs the certificate of death, that'll be everything."

"Of course, she needs to actually be dead before you can do that," the police officer said with a sad smile.

I plucked harder at the carpet, but couldn't get a grip.

Then I reached up and felt my hair. It was invisible while attached to my body. But what if it was no longer attached?

I grabbed a clump of hair and yanked at it. Pain flared up on my scalp and I gritted my teeth to stop myself yelping. But no hair came out.

I needed to start smaller. Separating a few strands, I gripped them between my finger and thumb. But when I yanked, they slipped through my fingers. I tried looping a few hairs around my index finger, but they weren't long enough to get a decent grip.

Sally-Taylor stood up and rolled her office chair back under the desk. "Let's speed up that process. We don't want her to still be alive when the doctor turns up."

I had to get out of here.

To beat them to old-Sally before they finished her off.

I grabbed my hair with both hands and yanked at it like a madman. If anyone could see me, they really would think I'd gone barking mad. I was literally pulling my hair out.

OW!

On the third attempt, pain flared in my scalp. I lowered my hands in front of my face and watched a small clump of hair materialise before my eyes. I held it out at arm's length, dangling it in front of the robo-dog, just as Sally-Taylor and her son stepped out from behind the desk.

Its eyes glowed as it focused on the clump of blond hair hovering in mid-air. I moved it from left to right and the robo-dog followed, so I dangled the hair in the direction of the door and jiggled it.

Suddenly, the robo-dog bolted forward like it had been shot from a cannon. I grabbed hold of its ear with my free hand to keep myself upright as we rocketed across the room. Sally-Taylor and the police officer leapt out of our way. But the door didn't. It loomed up in front of us, but the robo-dog didn't stop. Its eyes focused on the clump of hair, which was now waving wildly in the air. It leapt up and crashed into the door, nose first. The wood splintered as the robo-dog smashed through it like a cannon ball.

A split second later, I too hit the door nose first. But my nose was less like a cannon ball, more like an egg. There was a cracking sound as I fell backwards, landing with a thump on the carpet. Warm, sticky blood trickled over my lip and chin. I brought my hand to my mouth, then looked at it. At least I tried to look at it. All I could see was a gaping hole in the door.

Then the outline of my fingers appeared, all faint and red, like a ghostly hand.

Oh no! I had a nosebleed.

I spun onto my front and got on all fours. There was a drip, drip, dripping sound, and a patch of blood appeared on the carpet below me.

"What in heavens is that idiotic robo-dog doing now?" Sally's voice barked.

"I don't know," the police officer said. "It's been malfunctioning all day."

"Wait a minute... Is it bleeding?"

They both peered through me at the slowly spreading patch of blood on the carpet.

"It can't be," the Taylor twin said. "They replicated a police dog's mind, but its body is metal."

He stepped forward, squinting at the puddle on the carpet.

I needed to get out of there. Right now.

As the police officer bent over, I pushed myself up, holding my breath so I didn't make a sound. As he reached out towards the patch of blood, I dove through the hole in the door as though there was a swimming pool on the other side.

Unfortunately, there wasn't. My elbows slammed into the hard floor, followed by my jaw and already-sore nose. Then my foot scraped on the jagged wood, making me yelp again.

I rolled to a stop, my eyelids screwed shut but doing absolutely nothing. Droplets of blood appeared on the carpet beneath my face. Light shone through the hole in the door, and K10's eyes glowed further down the corridor. It let out a growl and charged towards me!

Its claws pounded the floor and my heart pounded in my chest. All I could focus on were its teeth as they glistened in the overhead lighting.

It was ten metres away.

Five.

Three.

I clambered to my feet and leapt out of the way as the robo-dog screeched to a halt, its claws gouging deep grooves in the carpet. It lowered its head and sniffed at the fresh patch of blood, as though picking up the scent of a wounded animal. Which was exactly what it was doing. And this wounded animal didn't want to become dog food.

I backed away from K10 and the patch of blood, but tiptoeing backwards is hard. Mainly because you can't see where you're going.

My butt cheek bumped into the corner of a dresser, and a vase toppled and fell off the edge.

I lunged for it with my left hand and, miraculously, caught it. That might be the first decent catch I'd made in my life. I think the only reason I didn't drop it was that my hand was sticky with blood.

The vase appeared to hang in mid-air while I marvelled at my newfound catching abilities. Then the robo-dog's head swivelled in my direction, its eyes glowing brighter as they focused on the gravity-defying vase.

Uh-oh.

It charged at me again.

I turned and launched the vase over my shoulder, in the general direction of the dog. The corridor lit up as the door swung open.

SMASH!

The vase exploded into a thousand pieces. I couldn't tell if it had hit the floor or the dog, but the tinkling and clattering went on for ages, followed by a ferocious command bellowed by the police officer.

"STOP! You foolish metal mutt! You're destroying the place!"

I skidded around the corner and stopped to look back.

Sally-Taylor and the police officer stood frozen in the doorway, but the robo-dog barely even paused. It leapt over the remains of the vase and headed right this way.

I turned and ran.

It was the only thing I could do.

But I was also running away from the mind-swapping machine.

25

The Chase is on

Up ahead of me, stairs led back to the common room.

I pinched my nose to stem the flow of blood, and took the stairs three at a time. The rapidly approaching clank of metal spurred me on.

I had to get away from it. To get back to the mind-swapping machine before they destroyed it and Sally's mind was lost forever.

But how could I get rid of this crazy robo-dog? Granddad's invention was too good. Too powerful.

And it was about to bite my butt at any moment.

When I reached the top of the stairs, the sound of chatter and TV game-show music came from up ahead. I put on a burst of speed and flew through the double doors into the common room.

Skidding to a halt, I glanced about, trying to figure out how to ditch my pursuer.

Most people sat around, like before, eating sandwiches and biscuits and donuts. The TV on the far wall showed Mum's favourite game show... The Chase.

How appropriate.

DaVinci lay on his back in the middle of the floor, his eyes only half open, tongue lolling out. It looked like he might have finally eaten more than he could handle.

As I rushed past him, DaVinci let out a little whine. I ducked behind a chair near the food table. What could I do? How could I stop that freaky thing?

The room went quiet, except for the tinny voices coming from the TV. The Beast was considering a question, the camera zoomed in on his face.

But I had a beast of my own to contend with. I peered over the back of the chair to see the robo-dog step into the room, its teeth glistening. Several of the homeless people gasped and backed away in terror.

Its eyes glowed, nostrils dilating.

Would the smell of coffee and donuts and life on the streets be enough to put it off my scent?

No.

Its eyes stared in my direction and it edged forward, heading right this way.

DaVinci leapt to his feet.

At first, I thought he would turn and bolt, as usual.

But he didn't.

He widened his stance, shifting his weight onto his back legs. Fur bristled along his spine.

A low growl rose in his throat, deep and menacing. And not at all like the cowardly dog I knew.

Go, DaVinci!

The robo-dog turned its attention away from me, squaring up to the real dog.

They locked eyes, and DaVinci's tail curled between his legs. He backed away, clearly losing his nerve.

My heart plummeted into my stomach.

What had I done now? At this rate, I could lose both Sally and DaVinci.

I had to do something.

But what?

I glanced around the room, frantically searching for something to help me destroy that stupid robot.

But this wasn't exactly a weapons depot.

I could hurl donuts at it. Or teacups. But nothing that might slow it down.

Up on the far wall was a red box with the word 'DEFIBRILLATOR' on the front. What if I blasted it with that? Except that's what Sally did to get it to swap minds when she saved me that time. And the last thing I needed was for DaVinci to swap minds with the robo-dog again. He'd caused enough chaos last time.

No. I needed something else.

A poker from the fire?

That was more likely to hurt my hands than K10.

The TV from the wall?

I wasn't sure I'd even be able to lift it by myself.

The robo-dog lowered its front legs, as though about to pounce.

DaVinci held his ground, but suddenly looked smaller. Helpless, even.

I stepped back and pain seared my butt cheek. Ow!

I'd backed into the tea urn. A massive silver thing, bubbling away with boiling water.

Maybe that might do it?

But I was completely naked. It could easily go horribly wrong.

DaVinci gave a yappy bark.

The robo-dog let out a deep dark rumble, like a cement mixer.

If I didn't do something, this battle would only go one way.

I grabbed the plastic handles on each side of the urn and lifted.

It was heavy. REALLY heavy!

If I could have held it in a bear hug, I'd have been okay. But bare-hugging boiling water would turn me into a walking blister.

I couldn't hold it at arm's length. The whole thing swayed and I staggered under its weight, crashing into a chair. All eyes turned this way to see the hot-water urn lurching through the air like a silver phantom. A very hot silver phantom.

$5000
K10

I twisted and, just as the urn tipped, I gave it a huge push, singeing my knuckles but lobbing it over the back of the chair towards the robo-dog.

It bounced off the chair's springy seat, its lid pinging off.

The robo-dog roared as a wave of boiling water surged down, crashing over it.

Steam hissed off its drenched metal body.

There was a sizzle.

A crackle.

Pop.

Its jaw dropped open as if going in for one final bite, but then, with a faint electrical fizz, its glowing eyes flickered and slowly went out.

The terrifying robo-dog stood still for a second, giving no signs of life. Then it toppled sideways and clunked onto the floor.

I'd done it!

I'd destroyed K10.

DaVinci came forward tentatively, sniffing at the fallen beast. His tail wagged, and he raised his head high, as though proud of his actions.

"Calm down, everyone," Nurse Hardy's voice boomed. "There's nothing to worry about. The situation has ... um ... been contained."

She turned to another nurse. "Eric, can you clean that up, please? And get rid of that … thing. I'll just finish with these two, then I'll be back up to help."

She nodded towards Jesus and Reggie, who were waiting by the door.

Oh no … they were the last to get their minds swapped. Then the machine would be destroyed.

I turned to beat them downstairs and almost tripped over DaVinci, who was sniffing at a droplet of blood on the carpet. He looked up, sniffing harder, his eyes widening. He knew I was here. But I didn't have time for his antics. I had to save Sally.

A large plate of sandwiches sat on the edge of the food table, so I reached over and gave it a tug. The plate crashed onto the floor and DaVinci gave one final sniff in my direction before pouncing on the free food.

I bolted from the room, squeezing past Nurse Hardy and leaping down the stairs.

There was no time to waste.

26

A Change of Mind

I rushed into the mind-swapping room and looked around. I needed to come up with a plan. Before Nurse Hardy got back.

The room was as I'd left it, except for one thing. The hospital bed containing the old lady—and Sally's mind—had gone. In its place stood another sturdy wooden chair with dangling straps.

Where had they taken her? Please let her still be alive.

I glanced at the dog-head mind-swapper that hung on the wall.

It hadn't been dismantled yet, so all was not lost.

But if I ever wanted to get my sister back into her own body, I'd need the thing in one piece. The problem was, the people who had to sit beneath the mind-swapping machine were getting further and further away from it.

And how was I supposed to get them back to normal if no one could see me? Okay, so if I found old Mrs Sally, I could wheel her here when no one was looking. But Sally-Taylor wasn't going to willingly sit beneath the mind-swapper again, was she? And I couldn't show myself to her. Besides the fact that I was naked and had no idea where my clothes were, she'd definitely recognise me. Thanks to Sally's haircut, she hadn't yet realised who she was. But if she saw me, surely she'd put two and two together.

And then what?

Who knew what she'd do if she realised she was in Sally Butterby's body? The teenager who lived across the road. Her plan to secretly pass her mind into a new body would be ruined.

But I doubt she would stop there. She'd probably run away in Sally's body. Or bodnap one of the other homeless people.

I paced the room, biting my lower lip, which was sticky with blood.

She needed to be stopped.

And with Mrs Sally knocking on death's door, it would have to be me who stopped her.

But how the heck was I going to do it?

This was too big a situation for me to fix by myself. I needed Sally. Or Mum and Dad.

Anybody!

Then the door behind me swung open, and Nurse Hardy walked in, followed by Jesus and Reggie. Jesus strutted in as though he owned the place, but Reggie hunched forward, frowning.

"You're the last two, then everyone's back to their old selves," Nurse Hardy said, ushering them both into a seat beneath the mind-swapper.

"I hope that don't bring no end to those sammies, Doc," Jesus said, reminding me they were still in the wrong bodies.

"Don't worry, Reggie, there's plenty more where they came from," the nurse said as she tightened the strap around his waist. "And Hey-ZEUS barely touched any, so you'll be able to fill up your own stomach, too, once you're back to normal."

"Bring it to me, Doc, bring it to me."

I retreated into the shadows as Nurse Hardy tapped at the keyboard with her index finger. The robo-dogs began their simultaneous growl.

As the grinding sound rose to its crescendo, the two men's eyes drooped shut.

Then they popped open, their expressions seeming to leap onto each other's faces. Jesus wore his usual grumpy frown. Reggie, on the other hand, beamed, his eyes twinkling.

"Back on me own turf," he said, patting his stomach. "And hungry for mo' sammies."

"If you head up to the communal area, you can help yourself," the nurse said. "You too, Hey-ZEUS. I've just got to do one thing, then I'll follow you up."

She was going to dismantle the mind-swapping machine.

I had to stop her. Now.

"Sure thing, boss lady, sure thing," Reggie said, strutting towards the exit.

Jesus followed him, head hung low.

Wait. Maybe Jesus would help me? He used to be a security guard. A very good one. And he knew I was invisible, so it wouldn't come as such a shock.

Nurse Hardy turned away the moment Reggie stepped out of the room, so I tiptoe-ran after Jesus. He stepped through the doorway and grasped the doorhandle, pulling it closed.

I put my foot in the way and the door thumped against my big toe. Jesus looked up, his eyes darting around suspiciously.

"It's me," I whispered. "Finn."

His eyes widened in understanding and he nodded.

"Guard the door and don't let anyone in or out until I say."

Jesus nodded again and pulled the door closed.

I let out a big puff of breath. I wasn't on my own any more. Jesus was here, helping me.

Which was kind of funny. I was supposed to be the one helping him.

A loud clank came from the other side of the room.

Oh no.

Nurse Hardy was standing on one of the wooden chairs, a spanner in her hand. The robo-dog's head closest to her had an ear missing. She was already dismantling it. I had to stop her, NOW!

I tiptoe-jogged across the room, the sound of my own heartbeat louder than my footsteps. The nurse grunted as she tried to turn the spanner.

What could I do?

She had no idea I was there, so I had the element of surprise. If I shouted in her ear, she'd either have a heart attack or fall off the chair. Perhaps both. But I didn't want to kill her. And I might need her help to get Sally back into her own body.

But what could I possibly say that would convince her to help me? Surely there was nothing. She'd never even seen me and had no idea who I was. Even if I took the collar off and tried to explain myself, would she listen to a bleeding naked boy who'd appeared in the middle of the room?

Not likely. She'd be more likely to lock me up somewhere with padded walls and plastic cutlery.

But she was the only one Mrs Taylor would listen to. I needed her on my side.

I frantically looked around the room, trying to find something—anything—I could use to convince her to help me. But there was nothing here, other than the two wooden chairs, the robo-dog heads, and the keyboard.

Wait ... the keyboard!

Nurse Hardy squatted down in the chair, looking into the robo-dog's mouth. The keyboard was right beside her. What if I...

No time to think. Just act.

I dashed over to the spare chair and perched my butt cheeks on its arm. Reaching out with my left hand, I typed 'Proceed with direct swap' into the keyboard.

The nurse's whole body tensed as the two robo-dogs roared to life. Her eyes widened, but she didn't move, probably because she didn't think there was anyone here to swap with. I leaned over so my head was underneath the other robo-dog, just as the roaring reached its crescendo.

The room turned wavy with static, like a TV losing reception, then the lights dimmed. Or at least, the room seemed much darker.

I looked around and realised I was squatting on a wooden chair. The other wooden chair. I closed my eyes and everything went dark. I had eyelids that worked! And I appeared to be alone in the room.

"What on earth...?" said a voice beside me. My voice, sounding much more high-pitched than it usually does.

I glanced down at a nurse's uniform.

It worked! My crazy spur-of-the-moment idea had worked. I'd swapped bodies with Nurse Hardy!

Nurse an Injury

My voice came from the chair beside me. "What the...? Why can't...?"

The poor nurse couldn't figure out what was going on. And that wasn't surprising. A minute ago, she'd had no idea anyone else was in the room. And now she was in their body—which happened to be invisible—looking at her own body, which was where she'd left it. Right beneath the mind-swapping machine.

I stepped off the chair and stood up tall, wiggling my long slender fingers and turning my hands over to examine them. On my left hand I wore two gold rings, one sparkling with tiny diamonds. Wedding rings, I think. Wow! I'm married!

Oh yeah ... to someone called Dave.

"This can't be..." my voice said.

And I could see why she'd think that. How the heck was I going to explain this? Whatever I was going to say, I'd need to say it quickly, before she freaked out. If she ran off, that would be the third person I'd lost in the last hour. And this one would be the most difficult to find out of all of them.

"Don't panic," I said, hearing the wavy notes of panic in my female voice. "My name's Finn and I'm Sally's brother."

Silence.

"Um... Sally's the one who's swapped bodies with Mrs Taylor. I mean, Mrs Taylor swapped bodies with her. But she can't have it. That's my sister. Well, it's her body. And she's only young."

The words tumbled out of me. I couldn't stop myself. I needed to explain everything.

"It's sad that Mrs Taylor is going to die. It really is. But she's old, and she's had a long life. Sally's only fifteen. Or is she sixteen already? I can't remember. But the point is..."

The door opened, cutting me off.

Jesus stood framed in the doorway, facing away from me. He clearly wasn't the one who had opened it.

"Hey-ZEUS!" I yelled. "Stop her. I mean, him!"

That didn't make a great deal of sense, so I added. "I'm Finn, and Nurse Hardy is in my body. Which is still invisible!"

Jesus rocketed forward, as though hit by a ghost train. He held his hands out and stopped himself on the far wall of the corridor, spinning around to face me. A determined look spread across his face and he squatted low, his arms spread out wide.

I jogged over to the door, glancing up and down the corridor. But it was deserted.

This was impossible. Granddad's collar was too good. Or bad. Whatever. How the heck was I supposed to find someone who was totally invisible?

Then I saw a drop of blood appear in mid-air at waist height. It fell onto the faded carpet and splashed out in a dark circle.

Without giving it a second thought, I dived forward. Pain erupted in my knees, hips, back, shoulders, wrists—pretty much everywhere—as I hit the floor and slid along, my arms outstretched.

Ouch. Hitting the floor hurts even more when you're old.

My fingertips brushed bare skin, so I stretched out and locked them around an ankle. My ankle!

"Get off me!" my voice cried, but I tightened my grip.

"Help me, Hey-ZEUS! I've got her!"

Jesus rushed forward, arms outstretched to stop Nurse-Finn getting away.

Pain flared in my hip, something solid in the nurse's pocket digging into me. I twisted my body so that it wasn't quite so painful, but that made it hard to hold on.

Fortunately, Jesus got hold of something, too. But she wriggled so much it was like wrestling an invisible alligator.

My fingers slipped off the ankle, so I rolled onto my side and tucked my free hand in my pocket to get rid of the lumpy thing. It was a bottle wrapped in cloth. Just as I was about to throw it away, the smell hit me. A chemical whiff that stung my eyeballs.

Wait! That was the stuff that Nurse Hardy held in Sally's face to make her fall asleep. And it was right there in my hand.

Jesus grunted. His arms were looped around like he was hugging an invisible tree. A very wriggly tree.

I pushed myself upright, my knees creaking and groaning.

"Keep hold of her!" I said as I twisted the lid off the bottle. I placed the bottle over the neck and tipped it upside down, just like I'd seen the nurse do with Sally. The only problem was, I couldn't see my target. I screwed the lid back on, slipped the bottle in my pocket, then held the cloth out in front of me, trying to find my own face.

The wriggling in Jesus's arms intensified, then my finger jabbed something damp and hard.

"OW!"

Oops. I think I poked her—or me—in the eye. My poor eyeball. But let's call that one payback!

Jesus let out an 'Oof!' and clutched his stomach, just as I shoved the cloth forward, dabbing it onto Jesus's chest.

No ... where did she go?

The slap of bare feet on the floor echoed along the corridor. Jesus and I glanced at each other, wide-eyed. How the heck were we going to find her now? We'd gone and lost my body. All three bodies that I needed. What an absolute nightmare.

Then, as if it really was a nightmare, the robo-dog stepped out of the furthest doorway, its eyes glowing.

What? How could that be?

I'd destroyed it. I was sure I had.

At that moment, the robo-dog's eyes lit up and it shot down the corridor towards me, its teeth glinting in the overhead light.

Instinctively, I raised my arms to protect my head from that vicious machine. But when I peered through the gaps between my fingers, I realised that this time, it wasn't coming after me. Well, not this me. It had skidded to a halt and opened its mouth wide, like it was about to swallow something whole.

My heart dropped to the pit of my stomach. That something was my own body!

28

Believe It Or Not

The police officer stepped out of the doorway and barked at the robo-dog.

"Heel!"

Then another identical officer—his twin—stepped out after him. "Stand down, Robert. That's an order!"

The robo-dog—or Robert—hesitated, its metal nose sniffing the air.

Wait a minute... I thought it was called Katy.

Oh.

I suddenly understood.

There were two robo-dogs. One for each police officer.

Of course!

Granddad had sold the plans, too, so they must have built more. And that also explained how they'd built the mind-swapping robo-dog heads.

Which was great. But it wouldn't prevent my naked body from becoming robo-dogfood.

"Help me!" cried a terrified voice in front of me. My terrified voice.

The robo-dog crept forward, getting closer and closer to the wall, narrowing the space between its jaws and my naked flesh. With no fear for my safety—or at least, the nurse's safety—I rushed forward, my arms spread out wide.

"Call that thing off!" I barked at the police officer, sounding even stricter and bossier than intended.

"Stand down, Robert!" the Taylor twin shouted again, but still nothing happened.

I spun around and shoved my butt in the robo-dog's face. I brought my arms out in a wide swooping arc, until they touched warm skin, and pulled invisible Nurse-Finn into a bear hug.

"What's going on?" said Sally's voice. I glanced up the corridor to see Sally-Taylor wheeling the hospital bed out of the far room. The bed containing Mrs Taylor's old body ... and Sally's mind.

My sister's eyes narrowed, staring at me. "Nurse Hardy? What are you doing?"

I hesitated.

But hang on. I was Nurse Hardy. I'd better act like it.

"There's an invisible boy on the loose," I said, trying to sound stern. "He tried to ... um ... stop me dismantling the machine. I've just caught him."

Nurse-Finn wriggled in my arms and I struggled to keep my grip.

Sally-Taylor and the police officers exchanged glances. Eyebrows rose and fell.

The robo-dog let out an especially loud growl, like rolling thunder.

"Get that beast out of here!" I barked. "Before it hurts this child. We don't want any more blood on our hands!"

Talking of hands, my right one was still clutching the damp cloth with that smelly stuff on it. I reached out with my left hand, feeling for Nurse-Finn's head, as though trying to protect it. I found hair, an ear, a cheek. Then I quickly pressed the cloth over the invisible nose and mouth. Nurse-Finn wriggled like crazy for a second, almost throwing me off, then she stopped and slumped onto me. I caught her under the armpits and lowered her onto the floor, keeping myself between my invisible body and the robo-dog.

"I'm done with this thing!" one of the police officers grumbled, rushing over. He typed something into the keypad on its butt. "How's it supposed to help me keep law and order when it's constantly out of order?"

The dog's eyes dimmed and it sat down neatly, the swirly pattern in the sphere on its head also dimming.

Sally-Taylor stepped forward, staring down at the floor in front of me.

"An invisible boy, you say?" Her eyes narrowed and she scratched the side of her head, looking exactly like Sally does when I play a prank on her. "If it's invisible, how do you know it's a boy?"

"Um... I... He..." I stammered, glancing at Jesus for support.

"He sound like boy," Jesus said, coming to my rescue.

"Yeah!" Then I remembered my earlier excuse. "He pushed me and told me not to destroy the mind-swapping machine."

Sally-Taylor moved her foot around beside me until it bumped into something. She squatted down, poking and prodding with her hands. "Fascinating!" she said, tilting her head to the side. "Do we know what's making him invisible?"

"Yeeaa... No!" I said, stopping myself from mentioning the collar. The last thing I wanted was for them to take the collar off and reveal Finn Butterby to Mrs Taylor and her sons. "I've no idea what could make someone invisible." Then I added, "Surely it's impossible!"

Sally-Taylor and her son exchanged glances again.

I held my breath, hoping I hadn't overdone it.

"It seems like nothing is impossible these days," Sally-Taylor said, sounding much older than she looked.

I glanced around me.

Amazingly, all the people I needed were in this one place. If I could lose the police officers and get into the mind-swapping room, I could fix this mix-up once and for all.

But how could I get rid of the policemen and the robo-dog?

Sally-Taylor looked up at her sons, who just happened to be roughly twice her current age. "Carry invisi-boy to my office and see if you can figure out who he is. And take that metal mutt with you. I don't want it causing any more havoc."

As the police officers bent down, each eventually grabbing an end of my body, Sally-Taylor turned to Jesus. "Be a dear, would you, Hey-ZEUS, and help me push my, I mean, the old lady, into the visiting room? The doctor will be here any moment."

Jesus glanced at me and I gave the slightest nod. He gripped hold of the headboard and started pushing. The police officers carried my body away, the robo-dog following at heel, its movements much clunkier and more robot-like than normal.

I couldn't believe my luck.

Old Mrs Sally lay motionless in the bed, but the monitor on the headboard showed a green line with regular peaks, so I knew she was still alive. Sally-Taylor marched off down the corridor ahead of me and Jesus.

I looked at my right hand, which still held the damp cloth.

This was almost too good to be true.

As Sally-Taylor walked past the door to the mind-swapping room, I rushed forward and placed my hand over her nose and mouth. Her eyes widened, her muscles tensing, but Nurse Hardy was considerably stronger than Sally, so I held her tight until she went limp in my arms.

Jesus pulled the door open, and I carried my sister's body into the room, her feet dragging along the floor.

By the time I had her in the chair with the straps done up, Jesus had wheeled in Mrs Taylor's old body and placed it underneath the other dog's head.

I'd done it. Sorry, we'd done it. With Jesus's help, I'd managed to get both bodies beneath the mind-swapper.

I just needed to type 'Proceed with direct swap' into the keyboard, and Sally would be back to normal.

29

Stop Dead

Jesus stood by as I stepped up to the keyboard.

I held my finger out, ready to type.

To my left, Sally's body was slumped to the side, her cheek resting on her shoulder. To my right, Mrs Taylor lay perfectly still, her skin grey and lifeless. The monitor on the headboard showed a mostly flat line, an occasional squiggle the only proof that she was alive.

I held my index finger out.

Just type the words, Finn.

'Proceed with direct swap.'

Then they'll both be back in their own bodies.

Do it now!

My eyes drifted to the monitor above the old lady's bed. The squiggles were getting smaller and further and further apart. They must have given her something to help her along. She could be dead at any moment.

I had to swap them now.

But I couldn't.

My finger just wouldn't move. I stood there, pointing at the keyboard as though accusing it of something.

Of what?

Then it hit me.

Murder.

That's what it was.

If I typed 'Proceed with direct swap' into this keyboard right now, I would be sending the old Mrs Taylor into a body that only had minutes to live. Essentially murdering her.

Okay, I'd also be saving Sally. But at the cost of another life.

And who was I to make that decision? I didn't get to decide who should live and who should die. No one should.

How would I sleep at night knowing that Mrs Taylor, former mayor and kind old neighbour, had died because of me?

There'd be a funeral.

The twins would be orphans.

All because I'd typed 'Proceed with direct swap' into the mind-swapper.

It was hard enough knowing that Jesus was homeless because of me.

That Mum and Dad no longer believed their own eyes.

But this? It was too much.

"What you waiting for?" Jesus demanded as I stood there with my finger poised.

"I... I ... can't do it," I mumbled. "I can't take responsibility for Mrs Taylor's death."

"But your seester?"

"I know, I know."

I looked at Sally's slumped body, a bit of drool dampening her shoulder. Then at the monitor with its fading squiggles.

I couldn't let Sally die, either. I had to do something, but not that. Not murder.

But I'd just knocked Sally-Taylor out with that stuff on the cloth. How was I supposed to wake her up? Was there an antidote to the smelly liquid?

She looked like she was sleeping. As if a dunk in cold water would wake her up.

That was it!

"Get me water!" I barked at Jesus. "Cold water. A whole bucketful."

Jesus nodded and dashed out of the room. I finally lowered my finger, staring at the monitor. A tiny squiggle came along.

I started counting.

One elephant.

Two elephants.

Three elephants.

Four elephants.

Five ele-squiggle.

Five seconds between squiggles. I'm no doctor, but that can't be good.

The door swung open and Jesus walked in carrying a stainless steel bowl. Well, it was like a bowl, but with a toilet seat-shaped rim.

"Is that ... a bedpan?"

"Ees all I find!" Jesus said, shrugging his shoulders as he passed it to me.

As I took the weight, freezing cold water sploshed over the edge onto my feet, slopping into Nurse Hardy's crocs.

I leaned over and sniffed the water. It smelled clean enough.

A small smile crept onto my face. If everything turned out okay, it would be fun telling Sally about this bit.

I stepped forward, held the bedpan high over Sally's head, then tipped it onto its side. A wave of water gushed out, hitting Sally right in the face, soaking her hair and clothes. Her muscles tensed and she hugged her arms to her chest, but her eyes remained closed.

More icy water splashed onto my legs and feet. It was seriously freezing.

Why wasn't she waking up?

30

Explain Away

I stepped forward and slapped my sister's cheek.

"Wake up!" I said in my stern nurse voice. "Right now."

I slapped her again.

Sally-Taylor groaned.

"Wuh?"

I glanced at the monitor. The squiggles had drifted further apart. Perhaps eight elephants.

I gave another slap for good measure and, thankfully, Sally's eyes fluttered open.

"Nurse Hardy? What's going on?"

"I'm not Nurse Hardy," I said. It was time for the truth. "I'm Finn Butterby—or Fingers—your neighbour."

Sally-Taylor squinted. "The blond boy? Who makes terrible lemonade?"

I nodded.

"What are you doing in Nurse Hardy's body?"

"I'm trying to stop you. That's my sister's body you're in right now. Sally. Sally Butterby."

Her jaw dropped open. "But ... it can't be... She ... she was homeless."

"No. She just pretended to be, so we could find out what you were doing with the homeless people. We were trying to rescue Hey-ZEUS!"

Jesus shuffled on his feet beside me, his eyes widening and his cheeks turning sunset pink.

"But ... my ... my own body..."

We all turned to face the bed on the other side of the mind-swapper.

"Is dying, yes. And I'm sorry. But you can't take my sister. I ... I need her."

My words hung in the air for a few moments, then the door swung open to reveal both police officers. Mrs Taylor's twins standing side by side, the remaining robo-dog behind them.

"What's going on?" the one on the left asked.

"Mother?" said the one on the right. "Are you okay?"

"I think you'd better come in," I said.

It looked like I had more explaining to do. But where to begin? It was one thing confessing to my sister's familiar face, but saying it to two police officers?

"I ... um ... it's ... er..." I said, unable to get the words past my heavy tongue.

"Oh, I'll do it!" Sally-Taylor said, rolling her eyes. "Boys, do come in."

I stepped aside as the two police officers entered the room, stopping between their mother's body and mind. The robo-dog clunked in after them, its footsteps echoing off the walls. The swirling pattern in its sphere was gone, and its movements were awkward and clunky. It looked like the real dog's mind was no longer in control.

Sally-Taylor spoke, spitting the words out as if each one tasted rotten. "That invisible boy is Finlay, the blond child from over the road. You know, the crazy family that drove into our house. Well, it's his body, at least. He's swapped with

Nurse Hardy here. And this," she gestured to her own body, "is his sister, Sally. Not a homeless person, after all. So, unfortunately, my dears, it looks like my time might be up."

"But surely..." began one twin.

"...there must be someone else?" his brother finished.

"Another body you can use?"

Sally-Taylor shook her head. "No. It's too late. I sped things along. My body only has minutes to live. At most."

We all turned towards the lifeless old body and the monitor above it. A faint squiggle passed by, like a scurrying bug. We stood there in silence, waiting for the next squiggle.

But it didn't come.

The monitor flashed with alerts and the speakers emitted a long piercing sound.

Her heart had stopped beating.

"Quick! Do it now!" Sally-Taylor said, her gaze drilling into me. As I stepped up to the keyboard, she turned her attention to her sons.

"Goodbye, my boys," she said, tears filling her eyes. "I'll always love you!"

This time I had no trouble moving my finger.

Jabbing letter by letter, I typed 'Proceed with direct swap' into the keyboard and the dog-head mind-swapper roared to life.

Instinctively, we all stepped as far away as we could.

The mechanical roar rose, drowning out the beep from the heart monitor.

My sister's body slumped forward. Then the mind-swapper fell silent, revealing the harsh beep once again.

Sally looked up, her wide eyes taking in the two policemen, Jesus, and me. "What? Where am I?"

"Sally? Is that you?"

She nodded.

I flung myself on her and gave her an awkward cuddle. At first I thought she wasn't cuddling back because of the chair's restraints. Then I remembered I was still in Nurse Hardy's body, and if there was a list of people you'd want to cuddle, she wouldn't be near the top.

"It's me," I said into her ear. "It's Finn. We did it. We got you back to normal."

Her cuddle cranked up a notch, like someone had hit the 'defrost' button.

I squeezed back.

Then I glanced over my shoulder.

Jesus stood to the side, staring at his shoes. The twins were slumped over their mother's bed, tears wetting their cheeks.

Oh.

Of course.

Sally was okay. But that meant that their mum had just died.

I let Sally go and stood up, not knowing what to do with my arms. After all, this was the hand that had typed into the keyboard. That had condemned their mother to her dying body.

The police officer on the far side of the bed examined the headboard. Beside the heart monitor were some of those resuscitation paddles. And next to them, an off switch.

The police officer hit it and silence seemed to leap up out of nowhere, offending my ears more than the beeping.

We all stood there awkwardly, not knowing where to look. The only sound was the occasional sob from one of the twins.

The robo-dog still sat in the middle of the room. Without the swirly pattern in its sphere, it too appeared dead.

I glanced between the sobbing police officers and the robo-dog. Then at the resuscitation paddles on the headboard.

"Wait a minute!" I burst out. "I have an idea!"

Operating System

"Quick!" I said. "Help me lift the robo-dog."

Jesus rushed over, clearly glad to have something to do. The two police officers were less enthusiastic. One of them wiped tears from his cheek, then the back of his hand on his trousers. They both stared at me with glassy eyes.

"Please," I said, clasping my hands. "This might just work."

Reluctantly, they left their mother's deathbed and came to the middle of the room.

"Everyone, grab a leg!"

We all squatted down and took hold of a metal leg. "Three, two, one, lift."

Pain shot through my lower back and knees as the robo-dog rose off the floor.

"Ees heavy!" Jesus groaned, the dog wobbling from side to side. For a moment, I thought it would topple on me, but we steadied it and brought it up to waist height. At least, it was Nurse Hardy's waist height. It almost came up to Jesus's chin.

"Over to the bed," I said, shuffling my feet in tiny pigeon steps to keep its sharp claws away from my shins.

"Quick!" Sally said, the straps of the chair preventing her from helping.

Tiny step by tiny step, we carried the metal mutt over to Mrs Taylor's bed. The two police officers grunted and huffed, their eyes only inches from mine. Their stale breath warmed my face, but I was already grimacing under the weight of the robo-dog.

"Spin it around. Lift it up."

We held it teeth first at the foot of the bed, then moved it up and along, until it was above Mrs Taylor's legs.

"Now, lower it down!" I said, and we placed it right on top of Mrs Taylor's frail body. The bed groaned under the weight and she folded in half, her head lolling to the side. If she hadn't already been dead, this would have killed her.

The robo-dog tilted, but didn't topple over, its head only inches from Mrs Taylor's face.

"Right, everyone step back!" I ordered, and they all obeyed. I wondered if they would have done so if I'd been in my own body. Probably not. Nurse Hardy was pretty scary.

I rushed around the side of the bed and grabbed the resuscitation paddles.

Would this even work?

The green line had been flat for a minute or two now. Maybe she was gone already.

A switch on the headboard said, 'Resuscitate', so I flicked it on and felt the hairs rise on the back of my neck. A static buzz filled the room.

Stretching my arms as far from my own head as I could, I placed the paddles on either side of the robo-dog's glass sphere.

Then I said "Clear!", like they do in the movies, and pushed the button.

The dog's body jolted and made a metallic grinding sound.

I kept my eyes on the sphere, but nothing. Just empty glass, like my savings jar.

"Clear!"

Another jolt and growl, but still no swirling pattern.

Dad always said third time's a charm.

So, I hit it again.

"Clear!"

"It's all right, Finn," said one of the twins.

"You tried," said the other.

I closed my eyes to trap the tears.

Why didn't it work? I was sure it was going to work.

Letting out a big puffy breath, I opened my eyes.

They instantly widened.

A swirly pattern filled the sphere. It started faint, but got brighter and brighter.

The dog raised its head. But not with a sharp, jerky motion. It was smoother. More controlled.

K10's eyes glowed bright yellow as it stared down at Mrs Taylor's lifeless face. When it looked up at the two police officers, the swirling pattern glowed even brighter.

"Mum?"

"Is that you?"

The robo-dog nodded! It actually nodded.

We'd done it! We'd saved Mrs Taylor after all. She'd be able to stay with her sons forever. And sit. And fetch.

Mrs Taylor was now a police robo-dog!

32. Riding the Wake

"Take these over the road for me, please, Finn," Mum said, nodding at an enormous platter of sandwiches. "And whatever you do, don't drop them."

I gulped. Seriously? No pressure.

I grabbed the tray at either end, my arms stretched out wide. For a second, I missed being Nurse Hardy. Things like this were much easier in an adult's body.

"Don't be silly, Mum," Sally said, swooping in and taking the tray off me. "We don't need ol' Butter Fingers dropping these on the carpet. You've already got enough to do."

She shot me a cheeky smile, then said, "Come with me, Finn. Make sure DaVinci doesn't trip me up!"

That was actually a pretty good idea. The moment we stepped into the hallway, DaVinci charged straight for us. I put myself in the way, letting him lick my face while Sally squeezed past with the tray of sandwiches.

The front door was already open, with people milling around in our garden, on the road, and spilling out of Mrs Taylor's house.

There were literally hundreds of people, all wearing suits or fancy dresses.

I grabbed DaVinci's collar, thankful it wasn't the vibrating invisible one, and slipped his lead on. Then I followed Sally out into the throng, DaVinci dragging me along and sniffing everyone's knees.

Jesus stood by our mailbox, shifting from foot to foot in a deep blue suit. A very different look from the dirt-smeared rags he'd been wearing a couple of weeks ago. He waved at us, and I raised my hand for a moment, until it was yanked away by DaVinci.

"Hi, Hey-ZEUS!" I said as we shot past him. "Where's Granddad?"

"He still at home! He finish one more thing then he come."

"Okay, thanks," I said, trotting after the dog. I still found it weird that Jesus was living with Granddad, but they both seemed to love it. It meant Granddad had even more help with DaVinci, and Jesus had a roof over his head. And a friend. The two of them got on really well.

Plus, Jesus was starting his new job soon. The Edith Taylor Homeless Shelter was officially opening next week, and it needed a security guard.

Sally weaved through the crowd with the platter, twisting and turning it to avoid bumping into people. Boy, was I glad I didn't have to do that. There'd be a Hansel-and-Gretel trail leading back to our kitchen, but with entire sandwiches instead of crumbs.

When we got to the kerb, DaVinci leapt off without looking, but this time it didn't matter. The road had been closed off, with cones and signs at either end, to allow for all the visitors.

I nodded and smiled at people as I passed, tugging at DaVinci's lead to stop him jumping up and slobbering on them. There were quite a few faces I recognised. Mr Kumar from the dairy. Dr Healy from the hospital. Even Mrs Higman, my teacher. It seemed like the whole town knew Mrs Taylor. Probably from when she was mayor.

When we arrived at the Taylors' front door, Sally angled the platter sideways and squeezed through.

I kept DaVinci's lead tight and followed her into the house. We smiled and thanked all the people who ducked out of our way, then Sally placed the platter on the dining table, next to the sausage rolls, chocolate brownies, and other delights.

Surely no one would notice if I had a chocolate brownie? Just a small one. I was reaching out to grab it when I noticed two bright yellow eyes staring at me. Mrs Robo-Taylor sat in the kitchen, eyeballing me.

Her teeth glimmered as her head swivelled from side to side.

On second thoughts, I decided to wait until after the service.

I spun around, and that's when I saw it. Mrs Taylor's casket. It sat on the far side of her living room, against the wall that Dad crashed into one time, pretty much turning her house into a drive-through.

The lid was off and her body displayed for all to see. She was so different to how she'd looked on the hospital bed, moments after she'd died. Her hair had been brushed, and she wore a sharp suit. It was like she was having a quick nap before joining the party.

I took a step closer, intrigued by how well she looked in death. She even had makeup on. And lipstick.

Suddenly, a growl came from the kitchen.

Mrs Robo-Taylor stood up and stared this way, as though ready to charge.

My stomach dropped a few storeys, my heart pounding against my ribcage, and I was just about to turn and run when I saw what she was looking at.

DaVinci had his front paws resting on the dining table and was gobbling sandwiches straight from the platter.

Oops.

Sally spotted him at the same time as me.

She leapt forward, and I yanked on the lead, dragging him away. A triangle of white bread protruded from his mouth and mayo was smeared up the side of his face. DaVinci swallowed the remaining bits of bread as I pulled him back. His fur bristled as he passed Mrs Robo-Taylor, but he wasn't quite as scared of K10 since his showdown at the homeless shelter.

I exchanged a nervous glance with Sally. We certainly didn't want the wrath of Mrs Robo-Taylor upon us. Or Mum and Dad, for that matter.

I watched Sally shuffle the sandwiches around the platter to fill the gap DaVinci had made. Surely no one would notice that.

"Finn!" Sally barked, pointing behind me.

Oh no! DaVinci had finished vacuuming the remaining breadcrumbs off the carpet and was now leaning into the casket, his tongue licking at Mrs Taylor's face.

I yanked at the lead again. DaVinci whined, then ran round in circles, wrapping his lead around my legs.

Sally grimaced, and we both peered into the casket. A wide smear of lipstick ran along Mrs Taylor's cheek and her eyeliner covered her entire eye socket like a bruise. And was that a dollop of mayo on her nose?

"I think we'd better see if Mum and Dad need any more help!" Sally said.

"Good idea!" I unravelled myself from DaVinci's lead and kept him close to my legs as we left the living room, passing other people going to pay their respects.

But when we stepped outside, it was clear that something was about to happen. Hundreds of people were milling around close by, looking at the Taylors' house. At the front stood the current mayor, the two Taylor twins in their police uniforms, Jesus, Granddad, Dad, and several men I didn't recognise. They all wore sombre faces and kept their eyes low as they marched past us in single file. DaVinci jumped up at Granddad, then at Jesus, who he could lick on the chin.

Eww. Lucky Jesus didn't know where that tongue had just been!

I pulled DaVinci back along the sidewalk, trying to keep him out of everyone's way. However, the moment we passed a lamppost, he cocked his leg and peed on it.

Why did I have to be on DaVinci duty with so many people around? He was a nightmare!

Then the crowd hushed and the robo-dog—or Mrs Taylor—stepped through the front door, her eyes glowing, claws clunking on the concrete.

The men followed Mrs Robo-Taylor out onto the street, the coffin held high on their shoulders. Fortunately, the lid was now on, so no one could see the dollop of mayonnaise on her nose.

How crazy is this? I thought, as Sally and I joined the procession that was following the pallbearers to church. DaVinci dragged me along, sniffing at everyone's heels.

Mrs Taylor—the robo-dog version—led her own funeral procession to church, her body following only metres behind her.

Surely it doesn't get more barking mad than that.

Yet it worked. The Taylor twins seemed happy. So did Mum and Dad and Granddad. Even Jesus was the happiest I'd ever seen him.

And it was all my fault.

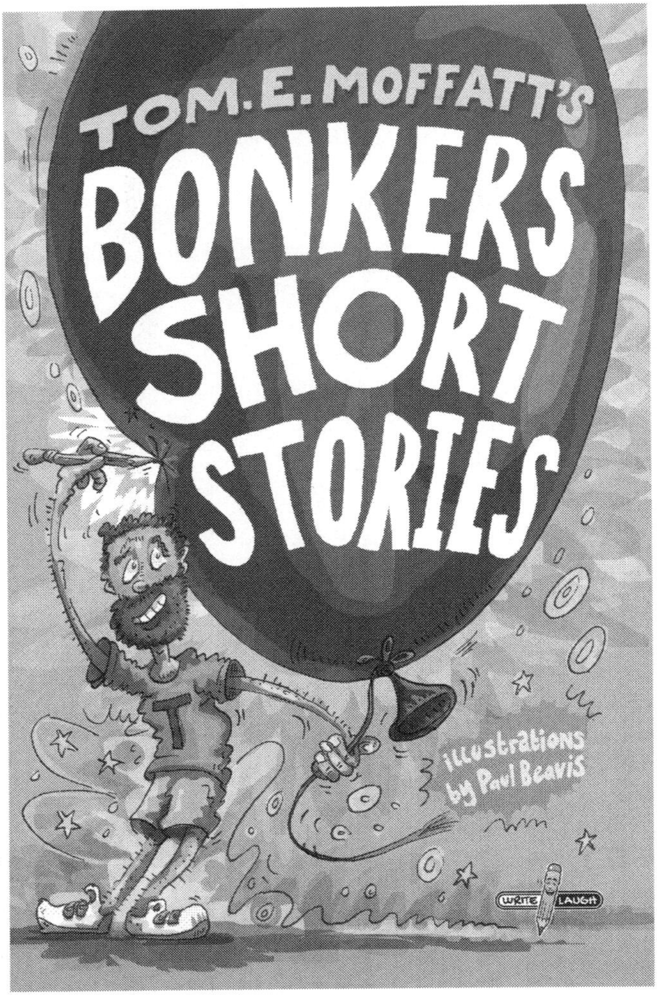

If you enjoyed *Barking Mad Adventures*, you'll love my *Bonkers Short Stories*. Download your free sample eBook now:

BONKERS SHORT STORIES

Volume 1:

MIND-SWAPPING MADNESS

A boy in a fly's body.

A toad waiting to be kissed.

Horses that know Morse code and aliens who hijack children's bodies. Has everyone gone completely bonkers?

Volume 2:

BODY-HOPPING HYSTERICS

Not all superpowers are a good thing.

Especially NOT if your mum has them. Or if they're fuelled by embarrassment. And what if you can't find your way back home?

Volume 3:

MIX-UP MAYHEM

Teleporting your mind across the Solar System.

Strangers using your body while you sleep. Underage time-travellers and remote-controlled baby-sitting devices. What could possibly go wrong?

I'm joking. You're joking. Everyone's joking in…
…TOM E. MOFFATT'S JOKINGDOM!

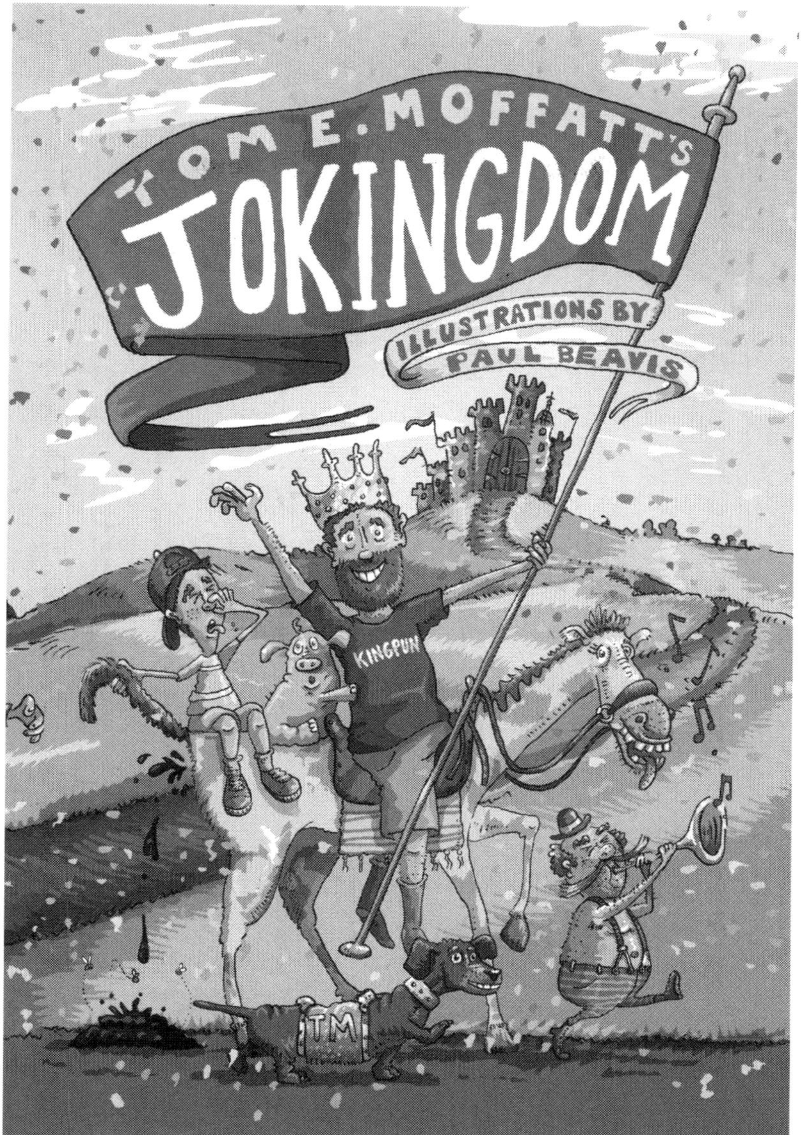

So, don your jester's hat and explore the realm of jokes at *www.TomEMoffatt.com/jokingdom*.

ABOUT THE AUTHOR

I'm Tom E. Moffatt, and I write jokes and fun stories for kids.

Lots of animals show up in my books, but if I had to choose between dogs and cats, I'd call myself a dog person. Just don't tell my cat, Nina. Although, to be fair, she's practically a dog. She follows me around, comes when she's called, and will eat pretty much anything.

I don't have a dog right now, but I've had several over the years—each one adding fuel to my Barking Mad adventures. And do you want to know one of my nicknames at school? Maddog Moffatt. Seriously. I've no idea why.

These days, I live in Rotorua, New Zealand, with my wife and three daughters. I spend my days writing, reading, and being followed around by my cat-dog. So far, I've published fifteen books—including joke collections and funny adventure stories like this one—all designed to get kids laughing and reading for fun.

For more information, silliness, and jokes, visit my website at www.writelaugh.com.

Made in the USA
Monee, IL
07 July 2026

56551521R00139